The Celtic Wisdom Tarot

The Celtic Wisdom Tarot

DEVISED BY CAITLÍN MATTHEWS
Illustrated by Olivia Rayner

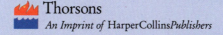
An Imprint of HarperCollins*Publishers*

*This pack is dedicated to Rachel Pollack,
Diva of the Decks, Juggler of Jokes, Spinner of Stories.*

ACKNOWLEDGMENTS

Thanks to John, Emrys, Barbara, and Felicity for their support. And to Olivia Rayner for converting my sketches into cards so clearly: blessings on her daughter, Eva, who was born between the Wisdom and Story Cards: *cumdach Bhandia órt, Iníon na Cartaí*! Thanks also to Rachel Pollack, Mary Greer, Dwina Murphy-Gibb, Anne Shotter, and to all my students who explore the vatic traditions of our land: thanks for accompanying me!

Thorsons
An imprint of HarperCollins *Publishers*
77–85 Fulham Palace Road
Hammersmith, London W6 8JB

Published in the UK by Thorsons 1999
1 3 5 7 9 10 8 6 4 2

Copyright © 1999 Godsfield Press
Text Copyright © 1999 Caitlín Matthews
Illustrations Copyright © 1999 Olivia Rayner
Designed for Godsfield Press by The Bridgewater Book Company

Photography: Guy Ryecart, Zul Mukhida

Special thanks go to Kay Macmullan *for hand modelling and help with photography*

Caitlín Matthews asserts the moral right to be identified as the author of this work.

A catalogue record for this book is available from the British Library.
ISBN 07225 36313

Manufactured in China

All rights reserved. No part of this publication may be reproduced, stored in a retrieval system, or transmitted in any form or by any means, electronic, mechanical, photocopying, recording, or otherwise, without the prior permission of the publishers.

Contents

The Celtic Realms 6

I LEAVES FROM THE SACRED TREE 9
The patterns underlying *The Celtic Wisdom Tarot*

II THE CIRCUIT OF LIVES 17
Introduction, background, and meaning for the Wisdom Cards

The Wisdom Cards 18

III THE SEASONS OF STORY 46
Introduction, background, and meaning for the Story Cards

The Story Cards 47

IV THE BRIGHT KNOWLEDGE 113
New spreads and interpretive suggestions for diviners

V THE PATHWAYS OF THE YEAR 132
A meditation course with the cards over the course of a year

Resources and Bibliography 144

The Celtic Realms

It was the Greeks who called the Celts *celtoi*: this may derive from a particular tribe or from a Greek word meaning "concealment". The Celts may seem a hidden people to us, for their myths have had less exposure than the Classical ones. Yet the ancestors and traditions of the modern Celts stem from the heartland of Europe and are the primary link between our agricultural and nomadic ancestors of prehistory and the subsequent civilization of the West. Their stories and myths are among the oldest remnants of our past, diffusing the mists of time and reconnecting us with our own soul's story.

Celtic peoples did not use writing, and their myths have been transmitted by oral tradition and through early clerical transcriptions. The ban on writing was upheld by the druidic class whose rigorous education involved years of memorization of genealogical, poetic, judicial, and other lore, and among whom the uttered word was supreme law, bond, and truth.

The Celtic Wisdom Tarot upholds that ancient oral tradition, which is here mediated through the visual and tactile format of the cards. In this way, each tarot reader who reads the cards for others keeps the immediacy of the oral wisdom tradition alive.

The tarot is popularly thought of as a "fortune telling" device, yet its 78-card format has a more fundamental use than this. *The Celtic Wisdom Tarot* offers the reader a portable oracle that can help clarify and give guidance in complex life-situations. It does not offer fateful outcomes, but helps the user awaken to the many possibilities surrounding a given situation and so act in a more empowered way.

Methods of divination were widely used by the Celtic peoples: auguries of animals and their movements, the shapes of clouds, forms of lot-casting, scrying in the elements, the wisdom of trees, and the prophecies of poets were all used to help guide decisions or to ascertain the will of the gods. Anything and everything existent might become the basis for divination, for the Celts believed that all things had soul.

The immortality of the soul was a central tenet of druidic belief, and the track of the soul through many lifetimes had its own distinct shape and pattern, which we see reflected in the intertwinings of Celtic knotwork and ornamentation.

The Celtic Wisdom Tarot follows the track of the soul's path through the 22 Wisdom Cards. These pattern into the sacred Triple Spiral, one of the primal symbols of the Celtic people. The Wisdom Cards do not depict individual stories, myths, or gods but rather the deep archetypes, aspects, and thresholds of the Celtic Otherworld. It is at these initiatory thresholds that all life is subject to mighty transformations.

The three cards shown below are chosen from the 22 Wisdom Cards. From left to right they are The Soul, The Guardian, and The Empowerer. These deeply archetypal images are key elements within the pattern of the sacred Triple Spiral.

0 THE SOUL

II THE GUARDIAN

VIII THE EMPOWERER

The 56 Story Cards reveal the more mundane features of life, depicting the rich variety of human experience through the tales and legends of the Celtic storytellers. These stories are codified into four families or suits: Battle, Skill, Art, and Knowledge, which were the four chief activities of the Celtic people. In these cards, gods, people, trees, ancestors, and animals reveal the rich nature of life.

When the Wisdom and Story Cards are shuffled together, the mingling of deep spiritual change and daily circumstance come about. This mingling of the cards reveals the circuit of the soul, which, in Celtic tradition, was seen to come forth from the cauldron of rebirth complete with its own innate qualities and gifts.

When we read the evidences of our soul's track, we attune to a deeper wisdom that has been hidden from us. The traditions of the *celtoi*, the hidden people, are potent keys of wisdom that can unlock the door of revelation for those who wish to read the mysterious and unwritten script of their inner lives.

To create this deck, I've drawn extensively upon my practical experience of working within the Celtic tradition over the last 30 or so years. The process has taught me more than I expected: when concepts and stories become visual and tactile in this way, something potent beyond expression is communicated. I am very grateful to the gods, spirits, and tree allies who have supplied the inspiration: for without them, this deck would not have been possible. May you find your own soul-path similarly accompanied with helpers, friends, and inspirers in whom you can trust! *Caitlín Matthews*

Augury of Battle is the first card in the Battle suit.

Quest of Skill is the tenth card in the Skill suit.

Courtship of Art is the third card in the Art suit.

Combat of Knowledge is the fifth card in the Knowledge suit.

To divination and the lot,
they pay as much attention as anyone.
The method of drawing lots is uniform.
A branch is cut from a nut-bearing tree
and divided into slips;
these are distinguished by certain marks
and spread casually and at random over
a white cloth.

TACITUS: GERMANIA X

LEAVES FROM THE SACRED TREE   I

Divination by Tree

Before writing, before the invention of paper, trees were regarded as oracles. Their tall trunks were long-lived witnesses of the ages; their spreading branches encompassed the seasonal wisdom of the turning year in leaf, blossom, fruit, and bareness. Their topmost branches penetrated the realms of the Great Above, while their roots reached down into the depths of the Great Below. Simultaneously growing between the manifest world of nature and the unseen realms of the spirits, trees were ambassadors of a deeper wisdom than humans could access alone.

Divination by tree was used extensively by our ancestors who recognized their qualities and codified emblems and symbols to represent their wisdom. In mainland Europe, sacred divinatory symbols called "runes" were inscribed on slips of wood, on objects, and on stones. In Britain and Ireland, the ogham alphabet was used for divination on wood and inscriptions on stone. The Celtic ogham symbols were under the aegis of Ogma, the God of Speech, just as the north European runes were under the protection of Odin, God of Wisdom. Though distantly related, oghamic and runic systems are quite separate. While both use a series of straight strokes to form each letter and each alphabet is 24–25 letters in total, there the resemblance ends.

Ogham was a method of inscription and augury, using a series of horizontal and diagonal strokes across the edges of stone monuments or squared-off lengths of wood. Inscriptions were read from bottom to top. It was a magical method of inscription used by the druids, seers, and poets, rather than a means of writing or communication.

One of the Irish ogham texts, *The Scholar's Primer*, describes the five ogham families as a tree to be climbed:

There are five ogmic groups. These are their signs: right of stem, left of stem, athwart of stem, through stem, about stem. Thus is a tree climbed, treading on the root of the tree first with thy right hand first and thy left hand after. Then with the stem, and against, and through it and about it.

(Auraicept)

In the creation of *The Celtic Wisdom Tarot*, I have asked each of the four chief *aicmí*, or families of trees within the ogham alphabet, to show me the visual symbols and oracular correspondences of the trees and the tarot. The cards in this deck are oracular leaves from those trees. The ogham content of this pack is quite subtle, visible only in the Wisdom Cards, but spreading its influence through the hidden veining of symbols. If you wish to work with the wisdom of the trees in more conscious ways, a method is suggested in Chapter 5. Alternatives to the ogham trees, for readers outside northwest Europe, are also given (see page 136).

The original 20 letters of the ogham alphabet have characteristic marks to identify them and are read from bottom to top. The top five letters were a later addition to the alphabet and are not used in *The Celtic Wisdom Tarot*.

AE	Phagos	Beech
IO	Iphin	Gooseberry
UI	Uilland	Honeysuckle
OI	Oir	Spindle
EA	Ebhadh	Aspen
I	Ioho	Yew
E	Eodha	Aspen
U	Ur	Heather
O	Ohn	Gorse
A	Ailim	Scots Pine
R	Ruis	Elder
Str	Straif	Blackthorn
Ng	Ngetal	Reed
G	Gort	Ivy
M	Muin	Bramble
Q	Quert	Apple
C	Coll	Hazel
T	Tinne	Holly
D	Duir	Oak
H	Huathe	Hawthorn
N	Nion	Ash
S	Saille	Willow
F	Fearn	Alder
L	Luis	Rowan
B	Beith	Birch

Using the Cards

In our own era, we no longer cut branches, twigs, or leaves from trees and use them in their raw state as oracles, but we do use their derivatives in a variety of divinatory ways. Chief of these is the use of tarot cards. If you've never used tarot cards before, please play with them as much as you can, looking at the images. Which cards attract you? Which don't you care for and why? Once you are familiar with the cards, try some of the simpler spreads. If you're an experienced tarot-user, familiarize yourself with the patterns and correlatives of the cards.

Each card's background and divinatory meaning is given in Chapters 2 and 3. In addition to the meanings for cards drawn upright or reversed, there is also an entry entitled "Soul-Wisdom." If you are having difficulty reading any card, refer to this and try to answer the question posed there: this may help reveal something else about the reading (see page 130-131.)

Always have a good question or issue to ask the cards: the clearer and more focused your question, the more you will learn about divination. The person who needs the reading should shuffle or mix the cards, and keep on shuffling while considering the question to be asked. He or she will know when to stop shuffling.

Spreads and sample readings are given in Chapter 4, along with suggestions for divining and interpretation. The cards do not have to be used solely for divination. Use them for storytelling, meditation, and self-clarification.

Reversed Cards

This deck shuffle uses cards both in their upright and reversed (upside down) positions. Not all reversed card meanings are opposite to their upright meanings: some intensify or lessen the message, others improve or alleviate the message. After you have mixed or shuffled the cards together, use one finger to push up a group of cards from a random place in the deck. Turn this group around until upside down, then reshuffle until they are thoroughly mixed throughout the deck.

Don't be afraid to deal reversed cards: like life, readings give us the rough with the smooth! Light is better appreciated from the perspective of doubt's darkness: light without shade is as tyrannical as night without day. As you place the cards on the floor or table, be sure to turn them sideways over rather than flipping them tail over head. If you are going to read for someone else, receive the pack of shuffled cards from the client the same way up as the client was holding them.

If you are unaccustomed to reversed meanings, then just use the cards without reversing a group to begin with. Then deal them as the cards appear. You might take note which cards come out reversed by accident in this method and see what difference this makes to the overall meaning. Break yourself into reversed meanings gradually.

Sometimes, as you shuffle, some cards or a single card will fall out: note these cards down and shuffle them back in. If they turn up again in the reading, then they are particularly significant, so pay them good attention.

This sequence shows shuffling a group of reversed cards into the deck.

The tarot deck after its initial shuffle.

Using one finger, push up a group of cards from within the deck.

Turn around this group of cards so that they are upside down, and return them to the deck. Reshuffle the deck thoroughly.

Care of the Cards

Some experts recommend somewhat precious and esoteric handling for your tarot deck, but such care is mostly common sense. The more you use and play with your cards, the more quickly they will become attuned to you. Many people like to wrap their cards in a cloth and/or keep them in a box. I still use a rabbit skin bought many years ago: it is soft, durable, and protective.

Before putting away the cards for a long period, your cards should be "cleared," or returned to their original upright order. This is a discipline that shows respect for the wisdom they contain. It returns them to their original sequence and breaks the mixture of patterns and stories they have been telling you.

After they have been returned to their original sequence, mixing or shuffling the cards is the discipline of seeking the story. In order to randomize the cards, deal the whole deck out in a line of seven positions, one on top of the other, and then reunite them in a random order into one deck. Give them to the client to shuffle thoroughly. In this way, the Seven Candles of Life are illuminated (see page 20) and you can seek out the wisdom of the story.

Diviner's Responsibilities

Divination by tarot is one of the sacred arts that must be practiced for real. Sacred arts are normally taught by oral and practical exposition, where the student naturally assimilates the kind of responsibility the diviner must have when he or she stands as mediator between the client and the spirits who give messages. Within my own teaching of Celtic wisdom, I ensure that students fully understand all their responsibilities and how to handle themselves in a world that generally regards divination as funny, entertaining, or deluded. I pass on the diviner's responsibility to you, with some suggested guidelines.

GUIDELINES FOR DIVINERS

1. To be a clear mirror of the ever-living truth appearing in the present moment.
2. To acknowledge the spirits and allies who are our divinatory partners: to credit them rather than to take credit yourself.
3. To uphold the weaving of the web of the universe: not to change it manipulatively.
4. To realize that there is cause and effect in this world: divination is based upon discerning the correlations between the apparent world and the unseen world.
5. To regard clients with respect and compassion: not to burden them beyond their capacity.
6. To find out and use personal methods of divination that are effective for yourself.
7. To find helpful pathways from the present moment into the future for living beings of goodwill.

May your experience of the Celtic Wisdom cards bring you to the heart of the oral tradition as a true oracle of wisdom!

Ethics and Divination

You will find your own methods and ways to read, but the most important thing is to divine with integrity. The ethics of divination are the essential foundation on which to build a healthy, well-run practice and ensure that you don't heap up trouble for yourself.

GUIDELINES FOR DIVINERS

1. Do not work for highly credulous or mentally unbalanced clients. Any words or advice of yours will take on portentous meaning far beyond your intention.
2. Do not use divination for obsessive life-guidance for yourself or others: this prevents the individual from discriminating and taking responsibility for personal actions.
3. Respect your spiritual allies. These may include a secret childhood companion, your guardian angel, saints, heroes, inspirers, and ancestors, as well as the spirits of trees, animals, and places. Seek advice from your allies seriously, and remember to thank them. Do not use divination frivolously, nor to ask things you could easily accomplish yourself. To do so is disrespectful to the powers from whom you seek help.
4. Do not seek to change the weaving of the universal web by spells, charms, or magic. Instead, change yourself, or show clients where they can change themselves, with the help of spiritual allies. Divination is a means of spiritual clarification not sorcery.
5. Do not read for those who haven't requested it or whose permission is not granted.
6. Do not use divination for entertainment or in inappropriate circumstances. However, learn and have fun with your cards.
7. Read the cards in ways that empower clients rather than make them depend on you or the cards. Be alert to the present moment, and your readings will be authentic and alive.
8. Don't divine when you are out of balance with yourself and the universe: the client should consult another diviner or come back another day.

Many diviners feel it is unethical to charge for readings, because they depend on spiritual powers for answers. But indigenous diviners worldwide accept something by way of reciprocation and thanks – be it coin, food, or services rendered. Besides, in our society, people do not respect things that are freely offered.

If your services are of a professional standard and you live by them, then please respect them and do not lay yourself and your art open to abuse. If you charge, have a sliding scale for clients in different circumstances and a reasonable standard fee that reflects the service you are offering.

THE CIRCUIT OF LIVES

I invoke the seven daughters of Ocean
who weave the threads of the sons of age.
Three deaths be taken from me,
three lifetimes be given me,
seven waves of surety be granted me!
May my seven candles never be extinguished!

INVOCATION FOR LONG LIFE: EARLY IRISH POEM
(translation: Caitlín Matthews)

The Wisdom Cards

The Wisdom Cards in this deck correspond to the 22 Major Arcana cards in traditional tarot decks. (For a complete list of the Wisdom Cards and their traditional tarot correlatives, see page 23.) Each Wisdom Card is indicated by a Roman numeral and its title, for example, XIII The Liberator (right). The original titles in traditional tarot decks derive from archetypes familiar to the medieval mind: some have dualistic overtones that make some cards attractive or desirable in a reading, while others are seen as unwelcome and malign. In *The Celtic Wisdom Tarot*, each card represents the archetypal qualities and powers that are found throughout the pan-Celtic tradition. These archetypes are manifest expressions of Spirit, which takes whatever forms it likes.

Each Wisdom Card bears a title that is descriptive of the card's function. The sequence and numeration of the Wisdom Cards do not imply that one card is better or more powerful than another: they are all vehicles of Spirit and so are not to be considered "good" or "evil."

Additionally the Wisdom Cards also depict the main 20 trees of the Celtic ogham tree alphabet (see page 11). Each Wisdom Card is allied with one of the trees whose Irish names were themselves the titles of each letter of the ogham alphabet. When old Gaelic speakers recited the ogham alphabet of letters they said, "Beith, Luis, Nion" meaning "Birch, Rowan, Ash."

The leaves of the Aspen – a tree feared in Celtic lore, and one of the main 20 trees of the ogham alphabet.

The numeral XIII indicates where The Liberator card appears in the Wisdom Card sequence.

The Liberator is one of the archetypal Wisdom Cards. It corresponds to the Death card in the traditional tarot deck. Here the Cailleach, a powerful goddess from Celtic lore, is shown.

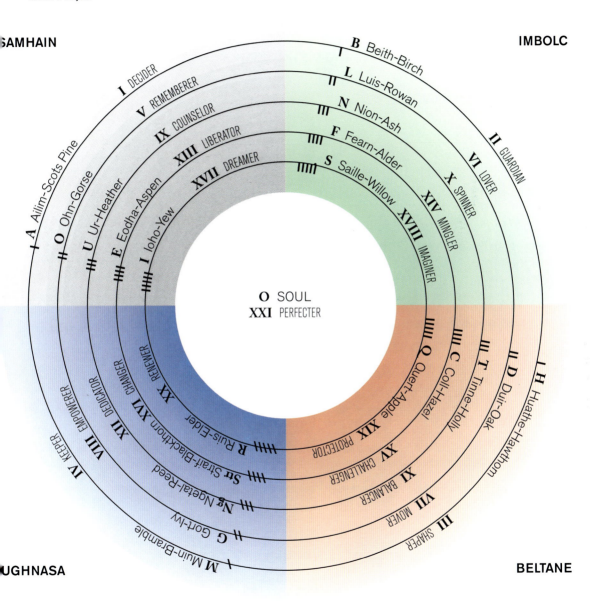

This diagram shows the Wisdom Cards and their corresponding ogham trees in relation to the four Celtic festivals of the year.

The Seven Candles of Life

The Seven Candles of Life are the sevenfold qualities that underpin the whole of life and illumine *The Celtic Wisdom Tarot*. Here they are shown with the cards that strongly manifest their influence. The card of the Soul encounters each of their illuminations as it moves on its path of experience.

0 The Soul

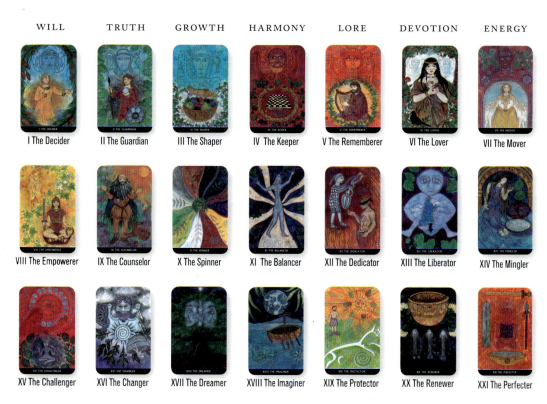

The Celtic Wisdom Tarot Triads

Each of the candles is illumined by three presences who maintain the existence of the universe. Here they are expressed in the style of the bardic triads – these are threefold sayings that encode the nature of their wisdom.

THE CANDLE OF WILL is illumined by the Three Unfailing Ones who uphold the universe: the Decider whose song never falters, the Empowerer whose deeds never fail, and the Challenger whose questions never cease.

THE CANDLE OF TRUTH is illumined by the Three Sparks of Wisdom: the Guardian who fosters the hidden truth, the Counselor who blesses the revealed truth, and the Changer who shows the shape of every truth.

THE CANDLE OF GROWTH is illumined by the Awakeners of Destiny who kindle the seeds of life: the Shaper who shapes the seeds, the Spinner who disperses the seeds on the many-colored winds, and the Dreamer who germinates the seeds in the darkest depths.

THE CANDLE OF HARMONY is illumined by the Three Fathomless Ones who maintain the order of the universe: the Keeper whose authority is boundless, the Balancer whose harmony is without measure, and the Imaginer whose depths none have plumbed.

THE CANDLE OF LORE is illumined by the Turners of the Wheel who keep the ancient lore in memory: the Rememberer who transmits the ancestral lore, the Dedicator who becomes one with it, and the Protector who welcomes the wise ones who pass beyond it.

THE CANDLE OF DEVOTION is illumined by the Three True Changers who renew love throughout the world: the Lover who kindles the Soul's desire, the Liberator who sets the Soul free, and the Renewer who rejoices in transforming the Soul.

THE CANDLE OF ENERGY is illumined by the Stewards of the Soul who imbue it with every grace: the Mover who motivates the Soul, the Mingler who bestows resourcefulness upon it, and the Perfecter who brings the living Soul homeward.

The candle of lore is illumined by The Dedicator, who keeps the ancestral lore in memory by becoming one with it.

The presence of The Protector illumines the candle of lore by welcoming the wise ones who pass beyond the ancient lore.

The Triple Spiral

The back of each card shows The Triple Spiral which, in this deck, represents the Soul's journey through the experiences, challenges, and inspirations of life.

FIRST SPIRAL OF REVELATION (cards I–VII) The Soul encounters the bearers of the Seven Candles of Life, the primal wisdom-keepers of tradition. Here the Soul's journey concerns the primal exposure to wisdom. We usually experience this spiral in our waking lives.

SECOND SPIRAL OF REVELATION (cards VIII–XIV) The Soul encounters the exponents of the laws of life, the ones who implement the wisdom of the Seven Candles. Here the Soul's journey concerns the practical and personal implementation of wisdom. We usually experience this spiral in our dreams.

THIRD SPIRAL OF REVELATION (cards XV–XXI) The Soul meets the deep Otherworldly guardians and participates in their initiatory revelation. Here the Soul's journey is concerned with the deepening and maturing of wisdom, and the Soul's identification with its principles. We experience this last spiral fully when the Soul is freed from the body.

After all three spirals have been experienced, the Soul (card 0) continues its *tuiriginí* or "circuit of lives."

The Wisdom Cards

	CELTIC WISDOM TAROT	**ORIGINAL TAROT TITLE**
0	The Soul	The Fool
I	The Decider	The Magician
II	The Guardian	The High Priestess
III	The Shaper	The Empress
IV	The Keeper	The Emperor
V	The Rememberer	The Hierophant
VI	The Lover	The Lovers
VII	The Mover	The Chariot
VIII	The Empowerer	Strength
IX	The Counselor	The Hermit
X	The Spinner	The Wheel of Fortune
XI	The Balancer	Justice
XII	The Dedicator	The Hanged Man
XIII	The Liberator	Death
XIV	The Mingler	Temperance
XV	The Challenger	The Devil
XVI	The Changer	The Tower
XVII	The Dreamer	The Star
XVIII	The Imaginer	The Moon
XIX	The Protector	The Sun
XX	The Renewer	Judgment
XXI	The Perfecter	The World

0
THE SOUL

OGHAM TREES *Birch and Yew*
OGHAM TITLES/LETTERS *Beith/B/Ioho/I*

DIVINATORY MEANING
UPRIGHT *A new phase or fresh start. Having vision or faith in oneself. Opportunity. Enthusiasm. Playfulness. Trust. A sense of protection.*
REVERSED *Halting or hesitation. Unable to heed instincts. A bad decision. Sloth. Irresponsibility. Immaturity. Carelessness.*

BACKGROUND The Soul is seen here as a young traveler on the path of his destiny. While he sleeps, his *riocht* or spirit-body goes forth in a dream to visit the immensities of the Celtic cosmos contained within the cauldron. The triple spiral etched in light over his head is emblematic of his physical vitality, his vocational commitment and his intelligence: in Celtic bardic lore, these are the three essential receptors for all inspirational wisdom. The triple spiral also represents the totality of the spiritual path, the three spirals of revelation that we all tread. The Soul was understood to continue after death, passing into different shapes or life forms upon its *tuiriginí* or "circuit of births." The Soul could enter into animal, plant, and elemental shapes, not just human ones. Birch and Yew are the first and last trees in the ogham families: the youngest and oldest trees.
SOUL-WISDOM Having respect for our Soul's purpose may look like foolishness to others. The power and vision of our Soul can only empower us when we acknowledge and manifest them. What is calling you to seek wisdom now?

THE DECIDER

OGHAM TREES *Scots Pine*
OGHAM TITLES/LETTERS *Ailim/A*

DIVINATORY MEANING
UPRIGHT *Willpower. Empowerment. Initiative. Accessing the imagination creatively. Plans ambitiously manifested. Concentrated effort. Discrimination. Competence.*
REVERSED *Weak-willed. Indecisive. Insecure. Manipulating others for one's own ends. Plans unrealized. Ineptitude.*

BACKGROUND The Decider shows Dagda, the Great God of the Druids, also known as Eochaid Ollathair (The Key-Bearing Great Father) and also as Ruadh Ro-Fessa (The Red One of Great Knowledge). The druids were the keepers of tribal wisdom and were able to arbitrate, divine from, and consult the spirits of the universe to discover solutions. By virtue of their attunement to the elements, rhythms, and patterns of the manifest world, and to the spirit allies of the unseen world, the druids were the mediators between the worlds. The Decider governs willpower and intention, and the druid is his exponent. The noble Scots Pine is native to Scotland and northern parts of Europe. Its distinctive red bark and high branches are easily recognized.

SOUL-WISDOM The Decider of Will sets the Soul on its journey. His unfailing song supports the Soul, reminding it of its true intention as it steps upon the path of its destiny. What is manifesting itself in your life now?

II
THE GUARDIAN

OGHAM TREES *Birch*
OGHAM TITLES/LETTERS *Beith/B*

DIVINATORY MEANING
UPRIGHT *Wisdom. Mystical vision.
Study and learning. Spiritual protection.
The inner life. Fostering potential.
Dreams. Intuitive insights. Ethical values.*
REVERSED *Ignorance. Surface knowledge.
Passivity. In thrall to illusions.
Values compromised. Superstition.*

BACKGROUND The Guardian shows the Goddess Brigantia, the Mistress of Truth, the "High One," who guards the land by truth, health, and creativity. The Goddess is known as Bride in Scotland; Ffraid in Wales; Brigantia in Britain; and Brighid in Ireland. The Romans likened her to Minerva and associated her with the Goddess Sulis, guardian of the city of Bath and matron of the only hot-water springs in Britain. The nuns of St. Brigit of Kildare, who acquired many attributes of the Celtic Goddess, maintained a perpetual flame in their sanctuary that was forbidden to men. The seer-priestess shown here is from one of the pre-Christian sisterhoods whose insight guarded the ways between. The Brighid's *crios*, a woven triskele of rushes, is a protective emblem that is placed in many households in Ireland today, especially around Imbolc. Birch is the first of the trees in the ogham family, the tree of beginnings, clarity, truth, and cleansing.
SOUL-WISDOM The Guardian of Truth prepares the Soul to seek for truth hidden in all places. The seer unfolds the patterns of destiny to the Soul. What is the source of your truth?

III
THE SHAPER

OGHAM TREES *Hawthorn*
OGHAM TITLES/LETTERS *Huathe/H*

DIVINATORY MEANING
UPRIGHT *Abundance. Wealth. Fulfillment. Reverence for the earth. Motherhood. Fertility. Loving guardianship. Value. Honor. Health. Harmony and wholeness. Emotional growth.*
REVERSED *Infertility. Poverty. Delay in accomplishment. Squandering of resources. Laziness. Inaction. Emotionally immature. Self-neglect.*

BACKGROUND The Shaper shows the Triple Mother, who was venerated by the Celts throughout Europe and was often shown bearing babies, fruit, grain, and bread. The Mothers maintain the fertility of the land, the life of its animals and people, and were often venerated as the guardians of the land's sovereignty. They maintain their loving watch over all life, transmuting the Soul from death into life. The three birds in this card are traditionally the companions of the Celtic Goddess of Life and Death: they are also forms that many semimortal or divine women take. Hawthorn is associated with the burgeoning of spring. Its clouds of white blossom appear on or around Beltane and its sexual scent reminds us of the May-revels when young lovers honor the time of life's renewal.
SOUL-WISDOM The Shaper of Growth gives life to all that is. The Mothers are the midwives of the Soul, nurturing it with qualities that enable it to respond to the good things of life. They also imbue the Soul with its instinct or mother-wit, the basic common sense by which we are protected and sustained. What spiritual nurture is your Soul seeking now?

IV
THE KEEPER

OGHAM TREES *Bramble*
OGHAM TITLES/LETTERS *Muin/M*

DIVINATORY MEANING
UPRIGHT   *Leadership. Administration. Stability. The harmony of orderly peace. Independence. Autonomy. Authority. Fatherhood. Intelligence. Benevolence. Self-assurance.*
REVERSED   *Disorganization. Instability. Dependence. Subservience. Ineffectual. Authoritarian. Domineering. Ruthless.*

BACKGROUND The Keeper shows Teutatis (Ruler of the People), a title that is recognized across the Celtic world. Local tribal stories about regional or national figures who fulfill this function include the legendary Irish king, Tuathal Techtmar, who derived from the earlier Celtic form "Teuto-valos" or Ruler of the People. The regional chieftains and rulers of every tribe all came under the fatherly eye of the Keeper. Regional rulership and the inability to combine forces under one leader often led to conflict. A strong ruler or over-king who could reconcile factions and galvanize tribes into a common purpose was invaluable. Arthur, the most famous war-leader to have borne the title of Keeper, was venerated for bringing long periods of peace and prosperity. Bramble, sometimes known as "vine," can be found growing in every kind of soil. It establishes itself and grows quickly and is one of the hardest plants to eradicate.
SOUL-WISDOM The Keeper of Harmony maintains the order of life. As the father of his people, he will not let them fall into chaos and dissension. What is the source of your own authority as a human being?

V
THE REMEMBERER

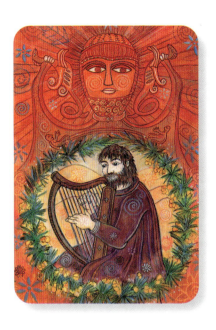

OGHAM TREES *Gorse*
OGHAM TITLES/LETTERS *Ohn/O*

DIVINATORY MEANING
UPRIGHT *Tradition. Mediation. Exposition of ideas. Remembrance. Genius. Performance. Spiritual counsel. Sacred lore. Faithful maintenance.*
REVERSED *Hidebound or conformist concepts. Muddling. Misinformation, propaganda or conspiracy. Forgetfulness. Adherence to narrow views.*

BACKGROUND The Rememberer shows Ogma, the God of Language and Eloquence and the creator of the ogham alphabet. In Ireland he is given the name Grianeinech (Sun-Faced). In Gaul and in other parts of the Celtic world, a native deity with a club was identified by the Romans as cognate with Hercules. The Gaulish Ogmios was said to be an old man who pulled men along tethered by chains that linked his tongue to their ears – the men were enthralled by his eloquence. This was the experience of any who heard the Celtic poet, the bard. Bards held the tribal lore in their memory: they were able to relate hundreds of stories and reached into their trained memories to speak authoritatively on legal, genealogical, and divinatory matters. Gorse is the glory of heathland. Its golden blooms appear early in the season and continue to color the landscape when winter is virtually at the door.

SOUL-WISDOM The Rememberer of Lore transmits the wisdom of traditions by which we all live. The essential lore that we need to keep ever before us is sung by the bard. What song is guiding you at this time?

VI
THE LOVER

OGHAM TREES *Rowan*
OGHAM TITLES/LETTERS *Luis/L*

DIVINATORY MEANING
UPRIGHT   *Choice. Attraction. Desire. Love. Friendship. Healing. Harmonious integration. Emotional freedom. Yearning. Speculating over a range of possibilities. Emotional entanglements.*
REVERSED   *Poor choices. Adolescent crushes. Quarrels. Choices affect health. Poor communication. "Pie-in-the-sky" hopes. Parental meddling or other interference in relationships.*

BACKGROUND The Lover shows Nemetona, the Goddess of the Sacred Grove, with her suitors. The *nemeton*, or sacred grove, was the place where druids and women of wisdom gathered. The dense woodlands that covered Europe were sanctuaries of mystery, sacrifice, and guardianship of wisdom. In Celtic tradition, love and rivalry are closely combined: a fact that is echoed in most of its love stories, which tell of rival suitors fighting over one woman. Although some tell how the woman is carried off by the winner, in many stories it is the woman who makes the choice. Lovers throughout the world often have a clear image of the one they desire. In Celtic story, this is often depicted as one with hair as black as a raven, skin as white as snow, and lips as red as blood. This theme of "the blood in the snow" is prominent in Celtic story. Rowan has a long tradition of being a magical tree that is used in spells but protects from sorcery.

SOUL-WISDOM The Lover of Devotion experiences the desire of life and makes the best choice for her future. Only the one whose image resides within our heart can be our beloved. Where is love in the situation?

VII
THE MOVER

OGHAM TREES *Oak*
OGHAM TITLES/LETTERS *Duir/D*

DIVINATORY MEANING
UPRIGHT   *Triumph. Success due to initiative and self-discipline. Obstacles overcome. Self-mastery. Being in control of one's circumstances. Prominence, fame, or greatness. Travel. Speed.*
REVERSED   *Defeat or failure. Ruthlessness. Success at others' expense. Loss of self-control. Addictive behavior. Egocentricity. Things careering out of control.*

BACKGROUND   The Mover shows Epona and the ancient nameless Goddess of the Chariot – a figure venerated across early Europe. The migrations of tribal peoples across Europe were by means of horse, cart, and chariot. During this nomadic phase, the image of the Goddess was carried about in a covered wagon or chariot, tended by her priestesses. Offerings were made to her in lakes and boglands. Epona is a pan-Celtic Goddess who is matron not only of horses but of passing over and through obstacles: she is also known as the one who opens the gates of the Underworld to the dead. In earliest times, it was believed that the chariot of the sun was borne by horses across the sky.

SOUL-WISDOM   The Mover of Energy motivates us with essential energy to act, just as the Goddess of the Chariot comes to activate the Soul. Which energies need to be harnessed now?

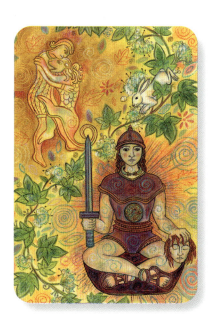

VIII
THE EMPOWERER

OGHAM TREES *Ivy*
OGHAM TITLES/LETTERS *Gort/G*

DIVINATORY MEANING
UPRIGHT *Fortitude. Courage. Energy. Resolution. Action. Defiance. Challenging that which is commonly accepted. Tireless efforts. The appetite to live life. Drawing on deep resources.*
REVERSED *Weakness. Vacillation. Dispiritedness. Indifference. Succumbing to prevailing influences. Failure of nerve.*

BACKGROUND The Empowerer shows Andraste, Goddess of Victory. "She Who is Unconquerable" was invoked by Queen Boudicca in her insurrection against the Romans. Part of Andraste's cult-practice included the loosing of a hare by the battle-leader. From the manner of its running and the direction of its course, it was possible to divine the outcome of combat. Female warriors were part of Celtic society: growing boys and girls were entrusted to them for their battle training. The Irish battle-leader, Fionn mac Cumhail, was raised by two such women, Bodhmall and Liath Luachra, while the hero, Cuchulainn, was trained by the supreme mistress of single combat, Scathach of Skye. The taking of heads in battle was not out of love of slaughter, but because the Celts venerated the head as the seat of the soul and as the link with ancestral wisdom. Ivy clings fast to any support, often overwhelming stonework and trees alike.
SOUL-WISDOM The Empowerer of Will gives us the courage to be strong and powerful in our lives, by using our own energies with intention. What powers lie untapped within you?

IX
THE COUNSELOR

OGHAM TREES *Heather*
OGHAM TITLES/LETTERS *Ur/U*

DIVINATORY MEANING
UPRIGHT   *Counsel. Inner guidance. Seeking professional help. Tactical or purposeful withdrawal to recoup energies or ideas. Pondering or planning. Discretion. Prudence. Proceeding carefully.*
REVERSED   *Bad advice. Refusal to heed wisdom or seek help. Isolation. Reliance on limited resources. Lack of accountability. Rash or foolish action.*

BACKGROUND The Counselor shows the Celtic god whom the Romans called Silvanus (He of the Woods). The figure of the one who returns to nature for his healing is seen in the Irish *Suibhne Geilt*, the British *Myrddin Emrys* (Merlin), and the Scottish *Lailoken*, all of whom live alone, with only trees and animals for companions. This deity was sometimes seen as a hunter or guardian of animals, a wise countryman who respected the rhythms of the seasons.
It was unusual for people in the pre-Industrial Age to seek out solitude for any long period of time. To be solitary was to be outside the tribe, outside the safety of family, beyond armed protection and cooperative help. Those who sought the wilds for their soul's sake were often seen as mad. Heather clothes the moors and hillsides, providing its sweetness to the bees and cover for the small animals and insects of this habitat.
SOUL-WISDOM The Counselor of Truth is a touchpoint of assurance and validation, reminding us that the three candles that illumine every darkness are truth, nature, and knowledge. What seeks to be born in the silence?

X
THE SPINNER

OGHAM TREES *Ash*
OGHAM TITLES/LETTERS *Nion/N*

DIVINATORY MEANING
UPRIGHT   *Destiny. Fate. Cause and effect. New cycle. Reaping what is sown. Auspicious circumstances. Unexpected change for better. Seizing opportunities. Respect for larger picture. Avoiding old patterns and mistakes.*
REVERSED   *Struggling against personal bent. Sequence of disruption or delay. Setbacks. Blaming. Reaping what is sown. Failure to note signs of change. Disregard of wider circumstances. Repeating unhelpful patterns or mistakes.*

BACKGROUND The Spinner shows the many-colored winds, which the Celtic peoples understood to have gifting qualities. The winds are under the aegis of the Ninefold Sisters, also called the Daughters of Ocean or the Daughters at the Back of the North Wind. As the gifting mothers of destiny, their breath impels each of us to find our gifts and use them. The skill of "reading the winds" also helped divine the kind of destiny one had, for the wind that was blowing when you were born defined your pathway in that life. This knowledge of the winds is hardly surprising in an island people whose weather can change dramatically even in the course of one day. Even today, many people are still experienced weather watchers. Ash is one of the straightest and tallest of trees, and has been famed as the world tree that connects the realms of the sky, the earth and the underworld.

SOUL-WISDOM The Spinner of Growth blows seeds into their appointed dance. It is a wise person who tests the direction of the winds before acting. What patterns are unfolding in your life?

XI
THE BALANCER

OGHAM TREES *Holly*
OGHAM TITLES/LETTERS *Tinne/T*

DIVINATORY MEANING
UPRIGHT *Equity. Justice. Receiving what is deserved. A fair outcome. Arbitration. Weighing possibilities. Vindication of truth. Honesty. Integrity.*
REVERSED *Imbalance. Injustice. Severity. Unfair treatment. Inflexibility. Prejudicial decisions. Lies and dishonesty. Abuse.*

BACKGROUND The Balancer shows the Goddess of Safe Passage, Nehelania, who is known as the "Steerswoman." She was invoked by all travelers, especially seafarers, and by those transacting business. Here we see her in her British, aspect, as Elen, the Goddess of the Ways, who is depicted as a Celtic dancer. Elen opens the ways, both roads and sea routes, as well as the dream-ways, giving free passage to those who take the trouble to map their own soul's route. This Celtic archetype was later absorbed in the stories about St. Helena, mother of Constantine the Great. Elen/Helen remained a popular figure in medieval legend, though her roadways became those opened by the cross of Christ. Holly here reminds us that life is ever-green and, despite its ordeals or difficulties, we can grow strong if we attend to our soul's purpose.

SOUL-WISDOM The Balancer of Harmony opens the ways but she also guards them. A life lived in full integrity is one that submits all its motivations and actions to truth first, rather than seeking to find out how truth may be bent to serve us. What keeps you in balance with the universe?

XII
THE DEDICATOR

OGHAM TREES *Reed*
OGHAM TITLES/LETTERS *Ngetal/Ng*

DIVINATORY MEANING
UPRIGHT   *Sacrifice. Serene submission to one's life pattern. Faith in integrity of one's actions. Initiation. Finding knowledge within. Dedicated service to higher cause or calling. Period of waiting or transition.*
REVERSED   *Selfish inability to relinquish. Unwilling or blind bondage to destiny. Unappreciated or useless sacrifices. Failure to commit. Pride or ego cause delays.*

BACKGROUND The Dedicator shows the Goddess of Sacrifice from the Gundestrup Cauldron (see page 44). Many stories speak of sacrificial caldrons that restore life to the dead, who return to fight again but are unable to speak; or of the cauldrons of initiation that utterly change those who drink. Archeological evidence of a bog-preserved body of a Celtic man revealed that he had been sacrificed by an ax-blow, by garroting, and by drowning: methods that involve earth, air, and water. For an unprepared person, such a death robbed the soul of its three sources of return through the elements: for a willing and prepared candidate, however, the threefold death was a sacrifice that integrated the soul into the universe, giving it the freedom to move through earth, air, and water.

SOUL-WISDOM The Dedicator of Lore makes a willing sacrifice to become one with the lore of his tribe, in order to be a transmitter of wisdom. This principle is one that many students, spiritual initiates, and heroes undergo today in order to be worthy lore-keepers. What duties arise from your beliefs?

XIII
THE LIBERATOR

OGHAM TREES *Aspen*
OGHAM TITLES/LETTERS *Eodha/E*

DIVINATORY MEANING
UPRIGHT *Change. Transformation. Removal of blockages. Clearing the way for liberating change. Letting go of old habits. Regeneration. Change of consciousness.*
REVERSED *Fear of change. Stagnation. Illness. Impasse. Stuck in old habits. Clinging to outworn ideas. Enforced removal.*

BACKGROUND The Liberator shows the Cailleach in her two appearances: the ancient Blue Hag, who formed mountain ranges by casting rocks from her apron, and the Sheila na Gig holding open her vulva, the womb and tomb of all life. The Sheila na Gig is a later image of a very early understanding: all beings now alive return to the earth through her on death. Through this two-way gate, we die to our personal life but are born to greater life. The Mountain Mother is called the Cailleach Bheare in Ireland and the Cailleach Bheur in Scotland. She is eternal and renews her youth through countless ages; she is the grandmother of all living, the lover of all life. She takes away what is outworn and renews it by her action. She is also the bringer of winter, the season where life is reborn and renewed. Aspen is a dreaded tree in Celtic tradition. Its wood was traditionally used by undertakers for making the measuring rod to measure the body of the deceased.
SOUL-WISDOM The Liberator of Devotion releases the Soul to unconditional love and liberation if we can humbly face and befriend death. What do you need to let go of?

XIV
THE MINGLER

OGHAM TREES *Alder*
OGHAM TITLES/LETTERS *Fearn/F*

DIVINATORY MEANING
UPRIGHT *Combination. Moderation. Coordination. Adaptation. Harmony. Compatibility. Fusion. Alchemical tempering. Subtle adjustment. Gifts of experience.*
REVERSED *Discord. Intemperance. Hysteria. Fragmentation. Hostility. Extremism. Clash of interests. Inability to work with others. Clumsy mishandling. Failure to learn from experience.*

BACKGROUND The Mingler shows Coventina, Goddess of the holy spring at Carrawburgh on Hadrian's Wall, which seems to have been popular with women who left offerings in return for safe delivery from childbirth. The deities of the waters were among the most primal spirits venerated by the pre-Celtic peoples: rites and offerings at ancient wells, springs, and lakes continue to this day throughout Europe, attended by those who seek the healing of the waters. Coventina is akin to another Celtic Goddess, Rosmerta (The Great Provider). Rosmerta is often shown churning milk into butter. Both Goddesses provide body and soul with suitable nurture, while transmuting opposites. Alder is a tree that grows with its roots in the water and was used for the creation of lake-villages and timber pathways over marshes.

SOUL-WISDOM The Mingler of Energy modifies our actions. It is by her vigorous churning that milk becomes butter, that our unformulated aspects become solidified. The ability to combine, to draw out the right decision or idea for the circumstances, lies in her gift. What is experience teaching you?

XV
THE CHALLENGER

OGHAM TREES *Hazel*
OGHAM TITLES/LETTERS *Coll/C*

DIVINATORY MEANING
UPRIGHT *Fear. Bondage. Extreme challenge. Misery. Obsession. Resentment. Role-playing for effect. Dependence. Manipulation. Humorlessness. Self-sabotage. Inability to realize goals.*
REVERSED *Understanding. Release. Breaking the spell. Respite from fears, obsessions, or worries. Recognition of the true self. Challenges are opportunities for growth.*

BACKGROUND The Challenger depicts the God Cernunnos below, while above, the Soul attempts to break free from the bondage of ancestral patterns. Cernunnos is the great Master of the Animals. His antlered head caused him to be demonized by Christianity and become associated with its antidivinity, the Devil. However, Cernunnos is actually an active opponent of restriction, fear, and oppression of all kinds; in legend he, and the figures who derive from him, lead the Wild Hunt to track down those who violate the laws of life. Here he holds the torc of the civilized human in his right hand and clasps the head of the primeval ram-headed serpent, emblem of renewal and animal consciousness, in his left. Hazel is considered to be the tree of poetic wisdom.

SOUL-WISDOM The Challenger of Will makes the Soul question what is accepted and find true release from fear. He speaks words of liberation and wisdom to those who can hear them. Those who hear only what they want to hear, and demand that others obey them, petrify the living stream of tradition into dead formulas. How are you limiting yourself?

XVI
THE CHANGER

OGHAM TREES *Blackthorn*
OGHAM TITLES/LETTERS *Straif/Str/Z*

DIVINATORY MEANING
UPRIGHT *Complete or sudden change. Alteration of the world as one knows it. Shocking or traumatic incident. Old habits overthrown. Breakdown. Routine destroyed. Revelation. Clarifying or cleansing event. Humility.*
REVERSED *Cooperation with disastrous influences. Refusal of help. Repression. Ignoring warning signs. The prolongation of suffering. Trapped in the past. Calamity. Squalor. Clouded motives. Hubris.*

BACKGROUND The Changer shows the God Taranis (The Thunderer), wielding his lightning bolt. The Romans associated Taranis with Jupiter and his thunderbolt. Taranis turns his wheel and everything is changed utterly. Victims dedicated to Taranis were stabbed to death as part of his sacrificial rites. The upturned caldron in this card appears in numerous stories where guests are invited to a specially built hostel by their enemies, only to find that the hostel is made of iron, that it has been heated from outside, and that there is no way out. When the mold is broken, we are forced to shapeshift. The sharp-thorned Blackthorn makes sloe gin, a potent ancient brew that has the effect of a thunderbolt.

SOUL-WISDOM The Changer of Truth uses shock tactics to shake all pride, smugness, and other inessentials out of us and to inculcate humility. He reveals interesting new shapes into which we can shift. What old habits, concepts, and structures have you outgrown?

XVII
THE DREAMER

OGHAM TREES *Yew*
OGHAM TITLES/LETTERS *Ioho/I*

DIVINATORY MEANING
UPRIGHT *Hope. Insight. Inspiration. Healing. Unconditional love. Optimism. Keeping faith. Dreams. Aspirations. Widening horizons. Promise and opportunity. A period of calm after storm. Recovery.*
REVERSED *Hopes dashed. Doubt. Short-sighted outlook. Poor health. Negative self-image. Pessimism. Insecurity. Self-doubt. Lack of trust. Swept into a spiral of activity.*

BACKGROUND The Dreamer shows the God Nodens, also called Iriel Faith (True Seer) and Nuadu Airgetlam (Silver-Arm). Nodens had a shrine at Lydney on the banks of the Severn in Glos, dedicated to healing and dream incubation. Pilgrims would invoke the healing deity and sleep the night in special cubicles or *abatons*; in the morning their dreams would be submitted for interpretation to the oracular priests of the shrine. Double-headed figures that look both ways appear all over the Celtic world. One head has the outward sight of the physical senses; the other, the inward sight of the seer or dreamer. This second sight in Gaelic is called *an dha shelleadh* or "the two sights." The star in this card reminds us of our origins, and is deeply encoded in every cell of our body. The tree of the Celtic Otherworld is the Yew, gateway to the Land of Promise. Its evergreen spines and red berries create the appearance of a tree on fire. It is the most enduring and ancient of trees.

SOUL-WISDOM The Dreamer of Growth gives us the necessary space to dream and discover ourselves, so that healing may come. What is the important source of refreshment in your own life?

XVIII
THE IMAGINER

OGHAM TREES *Willow*
OGHAM TITLES/LETTERS *Saille/S*

DIVINATORY MEANING
UPRIGHT *Imagination. Latent powers. Attunement to the rhythms, tides, and patterns of one's life. Unconscious influences. Dreams and visions. Introspection. Creative conception. Pregnancy.*
REVERSED *Illusions. Fear of the unfamiliar. Inflexibility and impatience with natural rhythms. Mental disturbance. Magnification of worries and problems.*

BACKGROUND The Imaginer shows the seascape of Manannan, the Irish God of the Otherworld and of the Sea. Like Odysseus, he is courteous and cunning, a companion to our soul's seafaring. He issues invitations to his realm to those who are worthy to seek his rich treasury. The golden-oared boat is an authentic image of the vessel used by those who made the *immram* or heroic voyage to the Blessed Islands of Manannan. On these voyages, mariners encounter the many islands that speak of the seafarers' life experience until they reach the Land of Women, a place of great blessedness and nurturing. Under the light of the moon, within the rhythm of the tides and currents, we discover our deep harmonious self. Willow is a fast-growing, water-loving tree. Its wood is adaptable for many purposes.
SOUL-WISDOM The Imaginer of Harmony sees deeply into the rhythms and patterns of the universe: an aperture upon the Soul that opens and closes as the moon waxes and wanes. Which of your natural rhythms are out of harmony?

XIX
THE PROTECTOR

OGHAM TREES *Apple*
OGHAM TITLES/LETTERS *Quert/Q/P/CW*

DIVINATORY MEANING
UPRIGHT Wholeness. Happiness. Attainment. Success. Simple joys and pleasures. Devotion. Fortunate meetings. Gratitude for life. Marriage. Good health. Openness. Sincerity. Safety after peril. Contented circumstances.
REVERSED Hollowness. Unhappiness. Broken engagements or relationships. Intolerance of shadows, such as inability to accept death. Political correctness taken to extremes. No chance to enjoy life. Lack of fulfillment. Maintaining the status quo.

BACKGROUND The Protector shows Belenus on the right and Dis Pater on the left, with the chalk-hill figure of Epona, making a strong protector triad upon the hillside leading to the Otherworldly Plain of Delight. Belenus (The Shining One) gave his name to the festival of Beltane, or "the fires of Bel," when May and the bright half of the year is celebrated. He has no known images in Celtic statuary but is reflected in the great solar head from the city of Aquae Sulis (modern-day Bath in England). Dis Pater was the Father of the Ancestors, the one who welcomes the dead to the summerlands. The White Horse of Uffington in England shows the dynamic, liberating presence of Epona, who opens the door to the summerlands. An introduced tree, the Apple became immediately widespread and has an important place in folklore.

SOUL-WISDOM The Protector of Lore brings everything and every being into the realm of simplicity and joy, where it can reveal itself and its gifts naturally. By aligning with our true self things go smoothly. Who are you in your true self?

XX

THE RENEWER

OGHAM TREES *Elder*
OGHAM TITLES/LETTERS *Ruis/R*

DIVINATORY MEANING
UPRIGHT *Transformation. Bringing matters to resolution. Releasing or forgiving. Freedom to act with full power or resources. A new lease of life. Recovery of essential focus.*
REVERSED *Denial of imminent change. Inability to admit faults or allow changes. Procrastination. Reproach for wasted opportunities. Stubborn self-justification. Little chance of cure. Failure to focus.*

BACKGROUND The Renewer shows us the Cauldron of Rebirth in its entirety for the first time. The Gundestrup Cauldron was found in a bog in Denmark, the fruits of a raiding expedition. This silver cult-vessel was custom-made for a Celtic sanctuary and depicts many of the major themes and deities of Celtic belief. The three hooded figures depicted here are called the *genii cucullati,* or the "Hooded Spirits," and appear in the context of renewal, healing, protection, and fertility. Here they appear as the triple guardians and initiates of the Cauldron, the spiritual sons of the Guardian Brighid, and as the three forms of the tripartite Soul. Having experienced the triple spiral of life, the Soul is made free and the *tuiriginí* or "circuit of existence" is renewed with deeper insight. Elder grows where it will, renewing the waste ground.
SOUL-WISDOM The Renewer of Devotion helps to deepen our compassion for the whole universe by bringing us to a better understanding of the patterns of our life and experience. Where is transformation imminent in your life?

XXI
THE PERFECTER

OGHAM TREES *All trees*
OGHAM TITLES/LETTERS *All letters*

DIVINATORY MEANING
UPRIGHT *Completion. Perfect or satisfying resolution. The end or finalization of a cycle. Successful achievement. Triumph. Self-respect. Synthesis. A sense of communion with all life. Clear self-expression and realization.*
REVERSED *Lack of momentum impedes endings. Failure to achieve. Inability to accept oneself, to allow changes or perfect closure, or to release potential. Inability to see the wood for the trees. Fixed or received views obscure self-essence.*

BACKGROUND The Perfecter shows the transfigured Soul meditating upon the experiences of the triple spiral. This Irish image shows the fourfold experiences of the seasons upon his breast, as powerful pathways of revelation. Within the center, the fourfold pathway is covered with the petals of realization. By use of all the powers of the ogham tree-letters, the Soul is free to seek and wield the four treasures of the Sword, Spear, Cauldron, and Stone – which are the emblems of the four suits of the Story Cards. The top of the Soul's head is no longer closed off but is open to the full range of spiritual influences, within the protection of the Soul's unfolding pathway.

SOUL-WISDOM The Perfecter of Energy brings every action into true alignment, enabling us to see and know the beginning and end of the Soul's story in brief but exquisite points of awareness, until it leads us homeward. The acts of our life are also the acts of our soul. What is the story of your soul?

THE SEASONS OF STORY

"How has Ireland been apportioned?"
"Not hard to relate: knowledge in the west, battle in the north, prosperity in the east, music in the south, sovereignty in the center."

THE SETTLING OF THE MANOR OF TARA
(translation: Caitlín Matthews)

III

The Story Cards

The 56 Minor Arcana cards of traditional tarot are called the Story Cards in this deck. The four suits are Battle, Skill, Art, and Knowledge, corresponding to the traditional tarot Swords, Wands, Cups, and Pentacles. These new titles have been selected from an old text, *The Settling of the Manor of Tara*, which details the division of Ireland. The number cards of *The Celtic Wisdom Tarot* deck depict stories and do not have proliferations of emblems on each card.

Each suit also represents a season and a direction; it has its own Otherworldly city and guardian and is represented by its own symbol. The four Celtic festivals mark the turning year: Samhain (October 31st) begins the winter – it is also known as the feast of All Saints and Souls and is the time of Halloween; Imbolc (January 31st) begins the spring and marks the lambing season and the feast of Brighid; Beltane (April 30th) begins the summer and is retained as May-eve; Lughnasa (July 31st) begins the fall with harvest-time. Celtic reckoning of time began with the eve or nightfall before the feast in question.

SUIT	SEASON	CITY	GUARDIAN	SYMBOL
Battle	Samhain	Findias	Uscias	Sword
Skill	Imbolc	Goirias	Esrus	Spear
Art	Beltane	Muirias	Semias	Cauldron
Knowledge	Lughnasa	Falias	Morfessa	Stone

The Court Cards

Each suit also has four additional "people" or court cards, which are called Woman, Warrior, Queen, and King, corresponding to the Page, Knight, Queen, and King in a standard tarot deck.

Women represent messengers who can clear the way and open new paths. Four dynamic women – Maeve, Arianrhod, Boann, and Airmed – open the way to the Four Treasures. They represent instinctive, pragmatic approaches and mediate the element of earth.

Warriors represent the challenge of their suit. Four warriors – Fionn, Gwydion, Oengus, and Mabon – guard the way to the Four Treasures. The warriors represent incisive, energetic approaches and mediate the element of air.

Queens bestow understanding of the qualities of their suit. Four Queens – the Morrigan, Rhiannon, Brighid, and Dana – initiate the seeker on the way to the Four Treasures. The Queens represent intuitive, emotional approaches, and mediate the element of water.

Kings are the protectors of the wisdom of their suit. Four Kings – Nuadu, Manawyddan, Lugh, and the Dagda – mediate the wisdom of the Four Treasures. The Kings represent dynamic approaches and mediate the element of fire.

WOMAN OF SKILL

WARRIOR OF KNOWLEDGE

QUEEN OF KNOWLEDGE

KING OF BATTLE

Four Court Cards are shown here – they correspond to the Page, Knight, King, and Queen in the standard tarot. Clockwise from the top they are Woman of Skill, Warrior of Knowledge, King of Battle, and Queen of Knowledge.

The Number Cards

The number cards are based on the storytelling genres of Celtic *seanachies* (storytellers) and are illustrated by Celtic myths and stories from insular traditions. Each card is numbered 1–10 and has its full title of story-genre and suit; for example, 3 Courtship of Art.

1. **AUGURIES** An augury is a prophetic encapsulation of the totality of someone or something. Like a seed, each of the Augury cards encodes the essence of its suit. Each of the aces are represented by the Four Treasures, which the Tuatha de Danann (the Tribe of the Goddess Dana) brought out of the Otherworld: the Sword of Nuadu; the Spear of Lugh; the Cauldron of the Dagda; and the Lia Fail, the stone of inauguration that belongs to the Goddess of the Land. Auguries represent primal beginnings and initiations.
2. **DIALOGUES** Dialogues involve give and take, listening and speaking: they fight for the development of the augury. The dialogues in this deck are famous ones: between Arthur and the Eagle; Merlin and Taliesin; Merlin and his sister; and between the poets Nede and Ferchertne. The Dialogues of the number two cards affirm and balance the Augury cards, revealing relationships and communication.
3. **COURTSHIPS** The seed of the Augury takes its first manifest shape in the threes. Each of the qualities of the four treasures of Battle, Skill, Art, and Knowledge become clear in the relationships of Cathbad and Nessa; Art and Delbchaem; Pwyll and Rhiannon; and Amairgin and the three Goddesses of Ireland. The Courtships explore the unity of the Auguries and make the first attempt to make them manifest. The threes indicate growth, expansion, and implementation.
4. **JUDGMENTS** These teach the essence of the Augury and bring it a stage nearer by the physical enactment of the principle. Setanta has to become a hound; Creiddelad's troublesome lovers have to learn patience; Cormac learns the strength of lies and truth; while Math teaches knowledge of being female to those who have abused a woman. The fours indicate stabilization.

5 **COMBATS** The lessons of the Judgments cause insecurity and require adjustment of attitudes. Cuchulainn's kinship and loyalty are tested when he sets to fight against his blood-brother; Niall's brothers fail to adapt to circumstances; brothers fall out and have a magical battle with the trees as combatants; and Macha is tested against the king's horses. The fives indicate change, friction, and testing.

6 **FOUNDATIONS** These cards demonstrate the harmony that surrounds the principles of each treasure: the warrior training of Battle; the smith-craft of Skill; the poet-craft of Art; and the druidic congress of Knowledge. The sixes represent balance, sharing, and security.

7 **ADVENTURES** These cards represent the exploration of the principles previously grasped in the Foundations. Owain and Arthur have a combat where gaming-pieces are also warriors; Manawyddan uses his skill to catch a shapeshifting thief; the Dagda wins back his harp; and Nera is dared to steal a corpse. The sevens represent promotion of ambition and ideals.

8 **ELOPEMENTS** These represent the realization of what is yet lacking, of the need for wholeness. Cuchulainn's soul is entranced by a faery woman; Midir rediscovers Etain through several incarnations; Pryderi and Rhiannon are abducted into the Otherworld; and Gwion elopes with the wisdom of Ceridwen. The eights represent the struggle to assimilate or succeed.

9 **REVELATIONS** These demonstrate the integration of the principle of their suit. Deirdriu realizes the worst when her lover is slain; Lleu and Blodeuwedd reveal their true natures; Conn realizes his destiny; and Tuan mac Carill recapitulates his life. The nines represent attainment and achievement.

10 **QUESTS** Quests represent the culmination of the principle augured in the Four Treasures (see page 49). Branwen is restored; Mabon is found; the Salmon of Wisdom is revealed; and the Cauldron of Annwfn is discovered. The tens represent endings and conclusions.

I AUGURY OF BATTLE

The following ten cards show the number cards in the Battle suit. These cards represent the links between the old Celtic myths and stories and their magical connections with the cards in the suit.

2 DIALOGUE OF BATTLE

3 COURTSHIP OF BATTLE

4 JUDGMENT OF BATTLE

5 COMBAT OF BATTLE

6 FOUNDATION OF BATTLE

7 ADVENTURE OF BATTLE

8 ELOPEMENT OF BATTLE

9 REVELATION OF BATTLE

10 QUEST OF BATTLE

Here are the Story Cards arranged around the year with the Wisdom Cards that guard and accompany their progress:

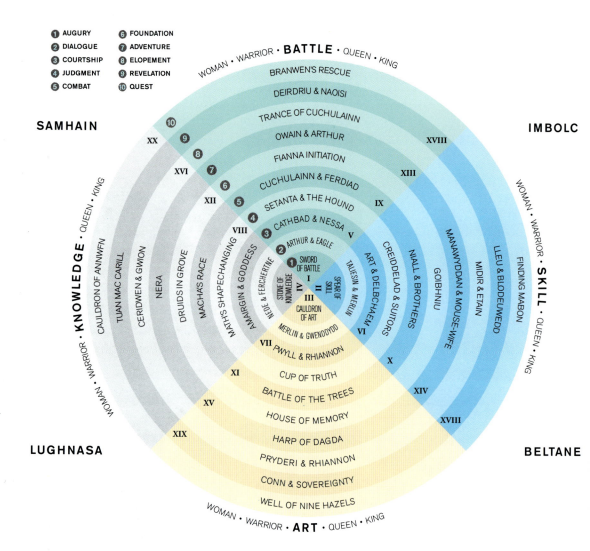

Suit of Battle

SAMHAIN *The Season of Winter*

AUGURY OF BATTLE

DIVINATORY MEANING

UPRIGHT *Battle or engagement. Power, strength, will. Achievement or advantage. Honesty and ethics. Self-determination. Vehemently clear or motivated. Active championship of causes. Conquest of difficulties. Breakthrough.*

REVERSED *Feeling powerless, victimized, or threatened. Insurmountable problems. Tyranny. Self-sabotage. Weakness. Submission. Ignorance or confusion. Hindrance. Mentally constrained.*

BACKGROUND We see the unconquerable power of the Sword of Nuadu: no man could escape its blade once it was drawn from its scabbard. The Sword of Nuadu came from the Otherworldly city of Findias, the Place of Brightness. Its guardian was the poet Uscias, the Praiser. Here we see the poet singing spells of victory upon the sword, much as bards and poets sang victory praises and songs of incitement to battle in times of war. The augury or prophecy given by the Sword of Nuadu is received upon the wings of the wind that blows freely throughout the world. The breath that animates all living beings enables the prophetic song to be sung. The spirit of the suit of Battle is heard most clearly through the element of air, from the regions of the sky, and especially in the winter season.

SOUL-WISDOM The Sword of Nuadu must be grasped firmly and confidently, with decisive vision and with honest motivation. How are you being called to engage more strongly with life?

2
DIALOGUE OF BATTLE

DIVINATORY MEANING
UPRIGHT *Reconciliation. Friendship or alliance restored. Temporary truce. Peace. Stalemate. A decision pending. Reviewing or resolving something. Seeing both sides of a situation. The mind considers the heart.*
REVERSED *Duplicity or treachery. Disloyalty of supposed friends. Indecision. Prejudice. Misrepresentation or lies. The mind rules the heart.*

BACKGROUND The Welsh *Dialogue of Arthur and Eliwlod* tells how Arthur met the spiritual form of his deceased great-nephew, Eliwlod. Eliwlod appeared in the form of an eagle and was renowned for giving good advice which, if followed, would ensure success. Here, Arthur consults him about how he should proceed. With the insight of the dead, Eliwlod tells Arthur to mend his ways, to commit himself spiritually, to act ethically, and to proceed with humility. This early Welsh Arthur was not, as in later medieval times, a ruler of chivalry and gentleness, but was instead known as "the Red Ravager." It is a common feature in Celtic lore for the soul to take the form of a bird. Cornish legend speaks of Arthur himself taking the form of a chough after his passing. There are many residual traditions concerning the symbiosis of birds and humans, forbidding the killing of certain species.

SOUL-WISDOM Rebalancing relationships and alliances when we have fractured harmony is a task we often neglect. What is needing reconciliation in your life?

3
COURTSHIP OF BATTLE

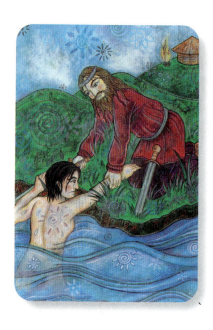

DIVINATORY MEANING
UPRIGHT *Sorrow. Wounded feelings. Separation or prolonged absence. Divorce or fracture. Pain or suffering. Old attitudes, situations, or beliefs need excision. Medical surgery. Rejection and its hurts.*
REVERSED *Living off old hurts or memories. Incompatibility. Revisiting painful memories. Minor separations. Repetition of old patterns. Feeling bruised. Low self-esteem.*

BACKGROUND In his youth, the Irish druid Cathbad spent some time as a freelance warrior. Among those killed by his raiding party were the fosterparents of Assa, the daughter of the King of Ulster. Assa, whose name meant "gentle," demanded that her father avenge her foster parents' deaths, but he couldn't because their assailants were unknown. In frustration and sorrow, Assa changed her name to Nessa or "ungentle" and roamed the wilderness as an outlaw in order to gather more information and kill the assailants herself. While she was bathing, however, Cathbad came upon her and entrapped her into becoming his wife. Despite this bad beginning, Cathbad and Nessa made a good match and were accepted by her father.
SOUL-WISDOM Nessa shows that there can be meaningful life after extremes of suffering. What sorrow or hurt is festering in your heart?

4
JUDGMENT OF BATTLE

DIVINATORY MEANING
UPRIGHT *Rest or respite. Recuperation or convalescence. Solitude. Retreat. Taking the pressure off. A space of meditation. Time to assimilate ideas and projects.*
REVERSED *Renewed activity. Careful progress or circumspect resumption. Employee strike action or other delay. Testing renewed strength or neglected abilities.*

BACKGROUND Young Setanta was too busy playing hurley to accompany King Conchobar to the feast given by Culainn the smith. When he did follow onward, it was long after Culainn had unleashed his fierce hound. Setanta wrestled with the hound and killed him. The company came out when they heard the outcry. When Culainn complained at the loss of his watchdog, Setanta promised to stand in the dog's stead and guard Culainn's property. The druid Cathbad judged that this was a fair recompense and, moreover, changed Setanta's name to Cuchulainn or "Hound of Culainn."
SOUL-WISDOM The achievement or winning of a thing, just like any period of great exertion, labor, or illness, is usually followed by a period of rest or assimilation. Where is such a space in your own life now?

5
COMBAT OF BATTLE

DIVINATORY MEANING
UPRIGHT *Conquest. Defeat. Destruction of others. Enemies seek your dishonor. Quarrels. Rivalry. No clear winner. Confused priorities. Spitefulness.*
REVERSED *Uncertain outcome. Loss at another's hands. Manipulative seduction. At the mercy of others.*

BACKGROUND When Queen Medb's army attempts to steal the great Brown Bull of Cuailgne, she attacks at a time when the Ulstermen are suffering from the curse of Macha (see Combat of Knowledge, page 103) and are too weak to fight. The sole defender of Ulster is Cuchulainn who proves undefeatable. Medb inveigles the reluctant Ferdiad, Cuchulainn's brother-in-arms, to fight against him. Both men are well-matched. Each day they fight; each night they tend each other's wounds. Cuchulainn's charioteer attempts to provoke some decisive action by mocking his master's skill, successfully goading Cuchulainn into his devastating battle-rage so that Cuchulainn thrusts his magical spear, the Gae Bolg, into his friend.

SOUL-WISDOM Hurting another always hurts oneself. Winning in such a way means that the fruits of victory cannot be enjoyed: conquest by dishonor robs the victor of honor. Which action, thought, word or intention of yours is having its effect right now?

6
FOUNDATION OF BATTLE

DIVINATORY MEANING
UPRIGHT *A journey or trip. Rite of passage. Moving on from unproductive areas. Changing attitudes. Successful transition.*
REVERSED *No way out from present difficulties. Delays and cancellations. Limited options. Having to make a virtue of necessity.*

BACKGROUND The roaming war-band of Fionn mac Cumhail, known as the *fianna*, was not open to all men to join. Only those who had proved themselves able in physical prowess, learning, and courtesy were accepted. Each member of the *fianna* needed to know the twelve books of poetry. In addition, candidates were tested for suitability by many difficult feats, one of which was to bury the candidate up to his middle in the ground and give him a shield and hazel rod to defend himself. Nine men would throw their spears at him from ten furrows' distance: only the candidate free of wounds was accepted.

SOUL-WISDOM Initiatory periods or rites of passage are required whenever we make a transition from one activity or age group to the next. The secret to making such transitions is to face them squarely. What threshold of opportunity or initiation awaits your engagement?

7
ADVENTURE OF BATTLE

DIVINATORY MEANING
UPRIGHT *Futility. Cheating. Stealing. Negative self-esteem. Self-sabotage. Undermining others or oneself. Heeding self-interested advice.*
REVERSED *Apology. Giving credit where it's due. Restoration.*

BACKGROUND In the British story "The Dream of Rhonabwy," Arthur and Owain ap Urien play a game of *gwyddbwyll*, a gaming board with pieces, like chess. When Arthur has the advantage, Owain's actual troops (called his "ravens") are beleaguered. Owain eventually bids his troops to raise their standard in the thick of the fray. When this happens, the fight goes the other way. Messengers come to Arthur, reporting that Owain's ravens are attacking his squires. Arthur requests Owain three times to call off his men, but Owain refuses. Eventually, Arthur crushes the golden board-pieces into dust and Owain's men lower their standard. Owain's mother is Morgen, the Raven Queen, and his standard is of magical assistance in this tale.

SOUL-WISDOM Whether we take something that is not rightfully ours, or whether we undermine our own abilities, the result is the same: we diminish ourselves. Winning by cheating or by sabotaging ourselves brings no victory. Whom are you seeking to deceive?

8
ELOPEMENT OF BATTLE

DIVINATORY MEANING
UPRIGHT *Restriction. Others decide on your behalf. Sickness. Hindered access. Addictions. Imprisonment. Stagnation. Isolation brings paranoia.*
REVERSED *Release. Clear perspectives arise once fear subsides. Depression lifts.*

BACKGROUND When a flock of unusual birds land on a lake, the women of Ulster all demand one. Cuchulainn brings back a pair for every woman except his wife, Emer. To appease her, Cuchulainn and his charioteer, Laeg, pursue a pair of birds yoked by a golden chain. Cuchulainn falls into a long, enchanted sleep for over a year, in which he sees the birds become women of the *sidhe* (the Otherworld) who strike him with horsewhips. He learns that one of them, Fand, has fallen in love with him. He sleeps with her and stays in the Otherworld for a month. A messy love triangle ensues, from which Fand finally withdraws. But the jealousy of Emer and the longing of Cuchulainn for Fand are unbearable. Druids give them a draft of forgetfulness to drink, and Manannan mac Lir, Fand's former husband and Lord of the Otherworldly realms, shakes his cloak between Cuchulainn and Fand so that they can never meet again.
SOUL-WISDOM Restrictive and stagnating prisons can be self-induced. Escaping from these requires us to ask for and to be able to receive help humbly and graciously. Which habits and attitudes are imprisoning and isolating you?

9
REVELATION OF BATTLE

DIVINATORY MEANING
UPRIGHT *Depression. Anxiety. Troubles pending. Cruelty. Miscarriage of child or events. Fear for another. Suffering. Burdens. Illness.*
REVERSED *Suspicion. Doubt. Fear of gossip. Shame. Patience required. Troubled situation begins to improve slightly.*

BACKGROUND When Deirdriu was still in her mother's womb, she cried out. Cathbad the druid divined that she would be the cause of great sorrow and destruction. Everyone clamored for her death as soon as she was born, but King Conchobar had her reared in secrecy, away from all men, to become his own wife. When Deirdriu grew up, she fell in love with Naoisi and they ran away to Scotland together. Under promise of amnesty, Conchobar lured them back to Ireland. Despite Deirdriu's warnings of a trap, Naoisi and his two brothers returned with her but were ambushed and killed. Deirdriu was finally married to Conchobar, but all she could do was bewail her loss. The king arranged to lend her to Eogan, the warrior who had slain Naoisi. On her way there, Deirdriu leaped to her death from the chariot.
SOUL-WISDOM Our anxiety about the future and our need for control can keep us confined in restrictive patterns of behavior. In your present predicament, where are the freedoms and alternatives?

10
QUEST OF BATTLE

DIVINATORY MEANING
UPRIGHT *Ruin. The worst is realized. Defeat. Hopes fail. Disruption. A hollow victory.*
REVERSED *Ruin deferred. Temporary gain. Overthrow of combatants or hostile forces.*

BACKGROUND When news comes that Branwen has been ill-treated by her husband, King Matholwch of Ireland, the men of Britain sail to rescue her. During a truce, it is proposed that Gwern, Branwen's son by Matholwch, should be made king of Ireland. But Branwen's brother, Efnissien, kills Gwern, and conflict ensues. However, Matholwch possesses a cauldron that revives his dead, and the British are soon outnumbered. The battle ends when the living Efnissien gets into the cauldron and it breaks. However, Bran, King of Britain, has been mortally wounded: he orders his own head to be struck off and buried facing the English Channel to serve as protection against invasion. Only seven men escape from the rout; they bring Branwen with them, but on reaching Môn (Anglesey in Wales) she dies from heartbreak at being the cause of so much slaughter.
SOUL-WISDOM After the worst is realized, we can begin the rest of our lives. This is not to disrespect the loss, nor to ignore the mourning, but to know that all things have their season, including ourselves: we do not share the same cycle as another being. What is the source of your greatest help in crisis?

WOMAN OF BATTLE

DIVINATORY MEANING
UPRIGHT *Someone who is intellectually astute; active, perceptive, and insightful; vigilant and diplomatic. Detached observer. The need to seize the moment incisively. Be alert to new ideas. Unexpected news.*
REVERSED *Someone who is cruel, critical, or sarcastic. Someone who intellectually questions everything. An impostor. Addiction to excitement. Unforeseen situations. Illness likely.*

BACKGROUND Queen Maeve (Medb in the Old Irish) was Queen of Connacht in Ireland. Having slept with many of the kings of Ireland, she took Ailill for her husband, because only he could meet her exacting standards: she could not accept any man in whom there was any meanness, jealousy, or fear. Her fiery, forceful personality is central to "The Cattle Raid of Cooley." Wanting the Brown Bull of Cuailgne for her own herd, she leads her army into Ulster and so precipitates an all-out war between the two provinces. She offers her daughter, Finnabair, to her champion, Ferdiad, if he can overcome Ulster's champion, Cuchulainn (see Combat of Battle, page 58). Maeve always remains wholly woman in her amours and keeps her lusty youthfulness by bathing in a magical lake.
SOUL-WISDOM Whatever the situation, Maeve is first into the gap. Ever alert to sudden change, she is quick to see how and where to act. What subtle changes are constellating around you now? In them lie clues to your action.

WARRIOR OF BATTLE

DIVINATORY MEANING
UPRIGHT *A strong-willed man of courage and heroism. He is fearless and quick to defend; sometimes overeager or wild, even fanatical. Time for forthright action and spontaneity. Championship of causes, defense of honor.*
REVERSED *A domineering tyrant. A rabble-rouser or starter of fights. Impulsive or conceited. Responding inappropriately or mistakenly through lack of judgment. Extravagance. Terrorism.*

BACKGROUND Fionn mac Cumhail was raised by two women who instructed him in weapons training and learning. Giving himself the name Deimne, he apprenticed himself to the druidic poet Finn Eces and learned the craft of poetry and obtained wise insight from eating the Salmon of Wisdom (see Quest of Art, page 93). Forever afterward he was able to reveal the unknown by biting his "thumb of knowledge." He rescued the honor of his father's war-band, the *fianna*, by finding its emblem, the Crane Bag – stolen by his father's killer. Because of his battle prowess, Fionn was made head of the *fianna* by King Cormac mac Art. Fionn's deeds and exploits are found in countless folk stories in Ireland and Scotland, in which he champions the weak and overcomes magical tyrannies and enchantments.
SOUL-WISDOM Sometimes we need to set aside our selfish concerns and personal agendas in order to step forward to help the common good. What requires our championship right now?

QUEEN OF BATTLE

DIVINATORY MEANING
UPRIGHT *A woman made wise by experience; sharp, analytical, and intelligent; autonomous and independent. Keen but fair. Someone who has overcome many obstacles. Strong principles. Dedication to personal liberty.*
REVERSED *A woman embittered by experience. Someone insistent on their own way. A gossip, delighting in others' misfortune. Narrow-minded or bigoted views. Harsh judgments.*

BACKGROUND The Morrigan (Great Queen) is the Goddess of Battle and catabolic change. With her sisters, Badb and Nemain, she assumes the shape of a crow or raven on the field of battle to pick at the flesh of the slain. She and the Dagda had a spectacular sexual congress over the Unius River in Connacht, in Ireland, and made an alliance to overthrow the invading Fomorians. She took the battle-will from the enemy and inspired the Dagda's people, the Tuatha de Danann, and proclaimed their great victory to the mountains, faery hosts, waters, and estuaries of Ireland. During the Cattle Raid of Cooley (see page 64), she came in her beautiful shape to offer her love, goods, and support to Cuchulainn but he, being in the thick of battle, curtly refused her. Thereafter she became his implacable enemy and returned in the shape of a raven to roost upon his body when he was dying.

SOUL-WISDOM The Morrigan can overcome all obstacles by her incisive power, bringing about transformation by dealing forthrightly with all that is stale and ripe for change. In which situation are you being called to make independent stands or opinions now?

KING OF BATTLE

DIVINATORY MEANING
UPRIGHT *A man who upholds rightful authority in high or professional office. Powers of analytical insight and original thinking give him authority, but do not make him authoritarian. Sound and respected adviser; impartial and fair. Commitment to the common good.*
REVERSED *Someone of corrupt authority. Misuse of power and intellectual prowess in cruel or sadistic ways: a "Godfather" or dictator. Mental arrogance. The unremitting face of authority. Unfair decisions made by faceless officialdom.*

BACKGROUND Nuadu was the leader of the Tuatha de Danann, but he lost his hand in battle. Because custom barred maimed leaders from continuing in office, he gave up the kingship for a while. Diancecht made a silver hand for him, which was later replaced by a hand of flesh and blood created by Diancecht's son, Miach (see Woman of Knowledge, page 109). This enabled Nuadu to return to his kingship. Nuadu subsequently ceded his place to Lugh, so as to contrive a victory over the Fomorian invaders when all other plans had failed. Nuadu's British counterpart is Nudd or Lludd of the Silver Hand, sometimes also called Nodons. A sleep-incubation temple dedicated to Nodons was discovered on the banks of the Severn River at Lydney in Gloucestershire, England. Nodons was the deity who brought true dreams.
SOUL-WISDOM Nuadu clarifies dilemmas and brings us clarity in decision-making. When resolution seems impossible, submit the problem to your dreams. What insights and experiences give you authority to act now?

Suit of Skill

IMBOLC *The Season of Spring*

AUGURY OF SKILL

DIVINATORY MEANING
UPRIGHT *Skill. Creation. The beginning of a project, enterprise, idea, or invention. Enthusiasm. Initiative. Energy. The joy of life. Sexual vigor. Conception. A journey.*
REVERSED *A false or bad start. Criticizing or not using one's potential. Journey deferred. Delays and difficulties. Failure of an enterprise.*

BACKGROUND The Spear of Lugh was brought from the Otherworldly city of Goirias: battle would never go against whoever wielded it. The guardian of the Otherworldly city of Goirias, the place of warming, was Esrus, the Kindler. The kindling of fire for the tribe was the sacred task of the people of skill. The Spear of Lugh, like the first rays of the sun, penetrates to the heart of all problems. The augury or prophecy given by the Spear of Lugh is received by all living things through the all-embracing power of the sun, which gives vigor, health, and joy to all. The spirit of the suit of Skill is received most clearly through the element of fire and in the season of spring when the creative fire returns to the earth.

SOUL-WISDOM Esrus kindles our enthusiasm and creative initiative. Wherever we cast the Spear of Lugh with this vitality, our life path grows correspondingly strong and decisive. Where are you being called to engage skilfully and enthusiastically?

2
DIALOGUE OF SKILL

DIVINATORY MEANING
UPRIGHT *A successful enterprise. Attainment of goals. Courage in undertakings. Personal fulfillment. Being more than equal to a challenge. Validating personal achievement.*
REVERSED *Venturing into the unknown. Loss of self-assurance. Plans do not work out. The reining-in or restraint of potential.*

BACKGROUND No one can restore the British prophet Myrddin (Merlin) to his right mind after a long period of madness brought on by exposure to the horrors of battle. He wanders alone in all weathers within the Caledonian Forest. It is only when the poet Taliesin comes to his old friend and relates to him the creation of the world that Myrddin is restored again. Taliesin describes the elements, the weather, the natural world, and its inhabitants, and so recreates the context for Myrddin to take up his life again. Myrddin's moment of reintegration comes about when the complex web of life is rewoven for him upon the skillful tongue of Taliesin: it is only when the fragmented soul is given a living, meaningful context that it can be reassembled.

SOUL-WISDOM When like-minded folk come together, or when challenge meets skill, the dialogue is assured and exciting. Where are your skills and goals being drawn together?

3
COURTSHIP OF SKILL

DIVINATORY MEANING

UPRIGHT *Rewards for achievement or enterprise. Hopes realized. Results through teamwork, partnership, or good relations. Negotiations. Help of a patron or benefactor. Practical skills. Business interests.*

REVERSED *The end of trouble. Wealth or achievements may disperse through lack of vigilance. Beware of help motivated by self-interest.*

BACKGROUND Art, son of Conn, was tricked by his stepmother, Becuma the enchantress, into going on a series of hopeless quests, including the finding of Delbchaem (Fair-Shape) from the Otherworld. But Delbchaem's mother, Coinchenn, knows of a prophecy that if her daughter is wooed then she herself will die, so she keeps strong protections around her daughter. Art defeats sea-monsters, a band of hags, a giant, and a poisoned cup; he overcomes Coinchenn and finally wins Delbchaem for his own. When Art returns home with his bride, Becuma is thrown out of Ireland and Conn cedes place to his son.

SOUL-WISDOM We hone our abilities by overcoming obstacles with skill and accepting assistance, so that we can be worthy to court and claim the goal that has motivated our efforts. What achievement lies within your sights? What help is being offered to you?

4
JUDGMENT OF SKILL

DIVINATORY MEANING
UPRIGHT *Completion of projects. Rest after work. Concord, peace, and harmony. Prosperity. Domestic wellbeing. Time to enjoy the fruits of labor.*
REVERSED *Increase and peace do not bring felicity. Lack of appreciation for the joys and benefits of life. Taking things for granted. Things remain unfinished.*

BACKGROUND Creiddelad, daughter of Llyr, was courted by two suitors: Gwythyr ap Greidawl and Gwyn ap Nudd. She was betrothed to Gwythyr, but Gwyn carried her off. Such was the ensuing upheaval and slaughter, that Arthur judged Creiddelad should stay in her father's house and that her warring suitors should fight for her every May Day till the end of time. Whosoever was the victor on that day should have her. Gwyn ap Nudd is associated with the powers of winter, and Gwythyr with the powers of summer. The eternal combat they have over Creiddelad is a mythic depiction of the yearly struggle between dark and light, cold and heat, decay and growth, which keep life in balance. Neither of these powers is good or evil: each is tempered and balanced by the other. Creiddelad is known in later medieval story as Cordelia.
SOUL-WISDOM The stability after a time of peace, prosperity, or harmony is continually tempered by the reality of change, growth, and decay. Is it time to enjoy the fruits of your efforts?

5
COMBAT OF SKILL

DIVINATORY MEANING
UPRIGHT *Arguments. Rivalry. Disagreements. Conflict. Overdefensive mechanisms disrupt things. Competitiveness. Obstacles to be overcome. Negative energy.*
REVERSED *Long-term disputes. Contradictions. Complex factors confuse issues. Do not let others call the shots.*

BACKGROUND King Eochaid had four sons by his queen, Mongfind, and a son, Niall, by his concubine, Cairenn. Niall and his brothers were tested by Eochaid to see which son should succeed him. The boys were sent out to hunt and fend for themselves in the wild forest. At sundown, they discovered that they had no water. In turns they went to fetch some, but each returned without it, looking shame-faced. Niall went last. He found that the only well was guarded by an ugly hag who refused to grant access to it unless she was given a kiss. The other boys had rather die of thirst than comply, but Niall embraced the hag, who turned into the most beautiful woman he had ever seen. She was the Goddess of Sovereignty and decreed that it would be Niall and his descendants who would inherit the throne, and not his brothers.
SOUL-WISDOM Within every dispute there is a solution, if we can set aside our personal point of view and see the whole overview. What is the kernel of truth and balance within your present dilemma?

6
FOUNDATION OF SKILL

DIVINATORY MEANING
UPRIGHT *Victory. Accomplishments or hard work honored. Good news. Advancement or promotion. Achievement of desires. Popularity assured.*
REVERSED *Deluded assumption of one's qualities or achievements. Failure to win; coming in second. Apprehension about victors and prime players in your field. Disloyalty of supporters.*

BACKGROUND Goibhniu is the Irish smith-god who is the patron of all skill and craft. He could make a sword or spear with three blows of his hammer but was once run through by one of his own spears. He was wounded by Ruadan, son of King Bres and Brighid, but merely pulled the spear out, ran Ruadan through, killing him outright, then bathed in the magical healing spring of Slaine. A similar story is told of his Welsh counterpart, Gofannon, who accidentally slays his nephew, Dylan, with a spear that is destined to kill the first thing to enter the forge. Goibhniu's magical ability to create weapons of virtue is echoed in the way he presides over the Otherworldly feast, the *Fled Ghoibhnenn*, at which he serves an ale that renders the drinker free of disease and death.

SOUL-WISDOM Recognition of achievement from others is good to receive, but it is also important to acknowledge our own worth and respect our own craft. What is your true skill in life?

7
ADVENTURE OF SKILL

DIVINATORY MEANING
UPRIGHT *Overcoming obstacles. Confrontation. Valor in the face of adversity. Tenacity and perseverance. Standing up for deeply held views. Defending integrity. Being in a position of advantage, however high the odds.*
REVERSED *Hesitancy and indecision. Embarrassment or anxiety caused by being at a disadvantage. Having the wind taken out of one's sails.*

BACKGROUND The kingdom of Dyfed falls under a mysterious enchantment, and Rhiannon and Pryderi are abducted (see Elopement of Art, page 91). Now Manawyddan and his daughter-in-law, Cigfa, will have to survive by their wits. Manawyddan's wheat fields are being robbed, but when he keeps watch on his last field, he sees an army of mice stealing the grain. He catches the slowest mouse as a hostage and builds a miniature gallows on which to hang it. In turn, three men come to bargain for the life of the mouse. Manawyddan is unyielding: he refuses to release the mouse until Rhiannon and Pryderi are released from their imprisonment and the enchantment upon Dyfed is lifted. It is then revealed that the mouse is really the pregnant wife of Llwyd ap Cilcoed, the Otherworldly man responsible for the enchantments. Faced with the possibility of his wife's death, Llwyd releases Rhiannon and Pryderi and restores the land of Dyfed.

SOUL-WISDOM When you are challenged, facing setbacks, or when you are asked to compromise your vision or belief, remember the source of your endeavor. What do you need to defend resourcefully?

8
ELOPEMENT OF SKILL

DIVINATORY MEANING
UPRIGHT *Freedom to move forward unimpeded. Speed. Activity. Swiftness. Messages in the mail. Speedy communication. Sudden progress. Hasty decisions.*
REVERSED *Jealousy. Domestic disputes. Harassment. Quarrels. Delay. Stagnation in decision-making.*

BACKGROUND Etain Echraide was married to the Otherworldly Midir. But Midir's first wife, Fuamnach, was furiously jealous and enchanted Etain first into a pool of water, then she turned her into a fly. Fuamnach then sent a wind that blew the fly into the cup of a woman, Etar, who drank it down and so conceived Etain as her own daughter, Etain daughter of Etar. The High King, Eochaid Airem, courted the reborn Etain to be his wife. Meanwhile, however, Midir had tracked down his beloved. Appearing as a rich stranger at Eochaid's court, Midir played a board game with him: the stake was to embrace Etain. Although Eochaid had ringed the hall with warriors, Midir seized Etain and together they rose up through the smoke hole; turning into swans, they returned to the *sidhe* (the Otherworld).

SOUL-WISDOM When energy, love, purpose, or motivation are given freely, results and returns are likewise speedy. Whatever you are waiting for, is delay the result of your reservations or suspicions?

9

REVELATION OF SKILL

DIVINATORY MEANING
UPRIGHT *Strength in opposition. Being in an attitude of defense against a situation or opponent who has attacked before. Obstinacy. Dogged opposition. Defending that which is dear – health, home, partner.*
REVERSED *Adversity. Weakness. Attacked when vulnerable. Failure to foresee opponent's intentions. Ill-health.*

BACKGROUND Lleu was given a wife, Blodeuwedd, who was made of flowers. However, she had no human desire for him. Instead, she wanted the warrior Gronw as her lover. To rid herself of Lleu, she asked him how he was fated to die. Lleu told her that he could be killed only by a spear that had been fashioned over a year, that he could be killed neither inside nor outside, neither on horse nor on foot. Only when he stood with one foot on the edge of the riverside, and with the other on the back of a goat, was he vulnerable. Blodeuwedd speedily instructed Gronw to make the spear, and then reproduced the circumstances of Lleu's fated death. Gronw cast his spear at Lleu, who changed into an eagle. When Gwydion (see page 80) restored Lleu to human shape, Lleu cast the spear at Gronw. After her lover had been slain, Blodeuwedd was then turned into an owl by Gwydion, as a punishment for her collusion.

SOUL-WISDOM Never disclose your weakness to your enemy. First discover your own weaknesses so as to be in the best attitude of defense. Where are you giving away power in your life?

10
QUEST OF SKILL

DIVINATORY MEANING
UPRIGHT *Refusal to delegate, burdened by responsibilities. Overcommitted. Stressed or pressured. Living up to impossible standards. Misuse of power.*
REVERSED *Burdens cast off by the easiest means, avoided or passed on to others. Mental instability or suicide. Victimization. Separation.*

BACKGROUND When Culhwch sought to marry the giant's daughter, Olwen, her father set him many impossible tasks, one of which was to find Mabon, son of Modron. Mabon was stolen three days after his birth and had been missing since before time was reckoned. Since human memory is no use, Culhwch enlists the help of Gwrthyr, interpreter of tongues. Together they ask the animals if they know of Mabon. The blackbird directs them to the stag, the stag to the owl, the owl to the eagle, the eagle to the salmon. The salmon brings them to the place where Mabon has been imprisoned for eons, along with all the men who have been upon the quest to release him.

SOUL-WISDOM When up against insuperable odds, remember Mabon is always waiting to be released: go to the heart of the problem and find the freedom before you become too isolated. If there are too many tasks or problems, how can you delegate or share them?

WOMAN OF SKILL

DIVINATORY MEANING
UPRIGHT *A person who is enthusiastic, loyal, and consistent; interested in others' wellbeing; warm and courageous, enjoying publicity and attention.*
An innovative or ambitious enterprise. Important news.
REVERSED *Someone who exaggerates or gossips about others; attention-seeking. Putting others at risk. Bad news.*

BACKGROUND Arianrhod's name may derive from the early Welsh for "Silver Tower," although the commonly accepted meaning is "Silver Wheel." She inhabits Caer Sidi, the revolving glass tower in which poets are initiated into the mysteries of inspiration: Arianrhod herself acts as the Inspiratrix and Muse of male poets. She came to her uncle Math's court in order to claim the role of virgin footholder. Math tested her by making her step over his magic wand. She immediately bore two children in full view of the court, for the wand had the ability to make the unseen manifest and so the fruits of her former lovemaking were born. She denied one of her children a name, the arms of manhood, or a wife of human stock. But she was tricked into giving him arms and his name of Lleu Llaw Gyffes by her brother, Gwydion. She is associated with the constellation Corona Borealis.
SOUL-WISDOM Arianrhod spins the thread of destiny from the tower of inspiration by her skill. Engage deeply with the things that move and interest you and your soul-thread will become the path under your feet. In what or in whom is your loyalty bestowed?

WARRIOR OF SKILL

DIVINATORY MEANING

UPRIGHT *A young man of strong opinions, impulsive and outspoken; vigorous and energetic; independent and spontaneous; exciting and creative. A dare-devil. A sudden departure or emigration. An overdramatic attitude.*
REVERSED *A choleric person, at odds with the world. Someone who is selfish, jealous, domineering, and sometimes violent. A sudden breakdown of relationships. Disruptions. Unstable circumstances.*

BACKGROUND Gwydion is the great trickster figure and shapeshifter of British tradition; he inherited his magical skills from his uncle, Math. He magically provokes battle to gain victory, and in so doing stands in a long line of druidic characters who use enchantment for these purposes. He creates horses and hounds out of toadstools, presents them to King Pryderi of Dyfed, and exchanges these for Pryderi's underworld swine. Gwydion manipulates his uncle into war in order to obtain Math's footholder, Goewin, for his brother, Gilfaethwy (see Judgment of Knowledge, page 102). In order to help his nephew, Lleu, win a name, manly arms, and a wife who is not of mortal stock, he makes shoes out of seaweed and a woman out of flowers. He is also the primary enchanter who causes the Battle of the Trees (see Combat of Art, page 88).
SOUL-WISDOM Gwydion turns disadvantage to his advantage by seizing opportunities. This skill is valuable, but it can also work against us if we approach life with a self-centered attitude. How do the difficulties facing you now provoke your passion and creativity?

QUEEN OF SKILL

DIVINATORY MEANING
UPRIGHT *A woman of practical common sense; sympathetic, warm, and powerful; influential and understanding; self-confident and courageous; resourceful, faithful, and supportive. Successful enterprises. Love of home and nature.*
REVERSED *A manipulative woman who misuses her power to get her own way; jealous, greedy, and unfaithful. Demands high standards in others. Resistance. Opposition.*

BACKGROUND The Otherworldly Rhiannon marries Pwyll after a difficult wooing (see Courtship of Art, page 86). She bears a child but, on that very night, the baby is stolen by an unknown agency. The midwives, fearful of blame, kill some puppies and strew the bones about Rhiannon's bed, swearing that she killed and ate her own child. Pwyll is unwilling to condemn her to death, so the judges order her to tell her terrible tale to all visitors to the court for seven years, and to bear them into the hall on her back. She is vindicated when her child and his rescuer come to court. After Pwyll's death, Rhiannon marries Manawyddan. Rhiannon's three blackbirds bring blessed healing to those fraught with burdens or sorrows. Her Irish counterpart is Cliona, who likewise has three birds of healing song.

SOUL-WISDOM Despite her wrongful accusation, Rhiannon maintains her integrity. Resourcefulness and courage reunited her with home and family. What does the voice of your common sense tell you about the situation now?

KING OF SKILL

DIVINATORY MEANING
UPRIGHT *A creative, enterprising man, always looking for opportunities to exert his full resources. His lack of ambition makes him helpful and compassionate. He relishes life and enjoys plunging into new experiences. Passion. Honesty. Marriage.*
REVERSED *A selfish man who insists on his own way and forces it on others. He is intolerant, prejudiced, and prone to excess and exaggeration; severe, suspicious, deliberately cruel.*

BACKGROUND Manawyddan, the brother of Bran the Blessed, married Rhiannon after Pwyll's death and became Lord of Dyfed. An enchantment fell upon their court at Narberth and they were forced to live by Manawyddan's craftsmanship: he made enameled saddles, shields, and gilded shoes. After the Otherworldly capture of his wife, Rhiannon, and their son, Pryderi (see page 91), Manawyddan's skill allowed him and his daughter-in-law, Cigfa, to live off the land and to overcome the enchantments. Along with Gwydion and Caswallawn, Manawyddan is named as one of "the three Golden Shoemakers." Manawyddan's Otherworldly realm was the Isle of Man, just as the realm of his Irish counterpart, Manannan, was in Emain Abhlach (the Isle of Arran in Scotland). Both of these Welsh and Irish figures are Gods of the Sea and of the Otherworld.
SOUL-WISDOM Manawyddan preserves the life of his family and makes a virtue out of necessity. Instead of waiting for circumstances to be perfect, we too have to draw upon our skills in order to bring our ambitions nearer to fulfillment. How do your skills serve your community?

Suit of Art

BELTANE *The Season of Summer*

1
AUGURY OF ART

DIVINATORY MEANING
UPRIGHT *Art. Abundance. Understanding. Love. Fertility. The beginning of happiness. Beauty. Emotional growth. Joy. Pleasure. Receptivity. Promise. Acceptance.*
REVERSED *Sterility. Feelings blocked. Change. Unrequited love. Joy clouded. Failure to foster or receive love. Starving in the midst of plenty.*

BACKGROUND The Cauldron of the Dagda came from Muirias: no company ever went from its nurture unsatisfied. The Otherworldly city of Muirias, the place of plenty, was guarded by the poet Semias, the Chanting One. She is seen here, singing spells of fertility upon the sacred vessel. The cauldron is a central feature of Celtic lore and bestows plenty, immortality, and inspiration in many stories. The augury or prophecy given by the Cauldron of the Dagda is received by all living beings through the bounteous moisture of the waters that quench thirst, cleanse, and heal. The spirit of the suit of Art is most clearly appreciated through the element of water, from the realms of the deep, and in the season of summer.
SOUL-WISDOM Semias blesses the way to abundance and growth in our lives. How are you being called to receive and grow?

2
DIALOGUE OF ART

DIVINATORY MEANING
UPRIGHT *Reciprocity of affection in love, friendship, or partnership. Sharing. Engagement, marriage, or contractual partnership. Passion. Mutual sympathy. Pledges and promises. Balance and harmony.*
REVERSED *Misunderstanding. Troubled relationships. Infatuation abates. Loss of harmony. Unequal behavior or expectations in a relationship. Divorce, breakdown, or separation.*

BACKGROUND The ancient dialogue between the British prophet Myrddin and his sister, Gwenddydd, tells how Gwenddydd comes to her brother in his madness and causes him to prophesy the course of the kingdom and proclaim its rulers. Gwenddydd yearns after her brother and is concerned for his welfare, doing all she can to bring him to himself again. After his restoration, she takes over his role of prophet and creates for him an Otherworldly observatory with many doors and windows, where he can retire and keep watch upon the land of Britain. This story devolved into the seduction and imprisonment of Merlin by Nimue in later medieval tradition.

SOUL-WISDOM The profound mutual affection between Myrddin and Gwenddydd creates an unusually strong relationship that abides, no matter what the circumstances. What is the basis of trust within your current situation?

3

COURTSHIP OF ART

DIVINATORY MEANING
UPRIGHT   *Happy outcome. Celebration of alliances. Recovery from illness. Healing. Merriment. Solace. Satisfaction. Good fortune. Hospitality. Satisfactory resolution.*
REVERSED   *Unhappy outcome. Loss of prestige. Too much of a good thing. Excess, dissipation, or indulgence. Beware of addiction. Unable to enjoy, or unaware of, the good things of life.*

BACKGROUND At the wedding feast of Rhiannon and Pwyll, Pwyll unwisely grants an open boon to a suppliant. The man is none other than Gwawl, Rhiannon's former suitor, who demands the bride as his own. Rhiannon wins some time for them, and instructs Pwyll what he is to do. At the wedding feast of Gwawl and Rhiannon, Pwyll arrives in disguise and asks for a boon. Gwawl guardedly grants one, select request: that Pwyll can fill his bag with food from the feast. But the bag is bottomless and the feast is disappearing, so Gwawl protests. Pwyll tells him that when a nobleman puts both feet into the bag and declares enough has been put into it, only then will the bag be full. Too impatient for caution, Gwawl complies and finds himself bound tightly into the bag and beaten with sticks. Pwyll promises to release him if he will relinquish all claim on Rhiannon. Pwyll and Rhiannon can then be married.

SOUL-WISDOM Closely observe the laws of cause and effect and don't do things you will later on come to regret. What stands in the way of a good outcome for you now?

4
JUDGMENT OF ART

DIVINATORY MEANING
UPRIGHT *Weariness. Surfeit. Everything bores, palls, or disgusts. Apathy. Reexamination of lifestyle. Dissatisfaction with life. Experience embitters.*
REVERSED *New possibilities, relationships, approaches, or realizations. Fresh ambitions enliven. Reawakening to life's riches.*

BACKGROUND The Irish King Cormac went into the Land of Promise in order to rescue his wife and family. He saw many wonders there, including a miraculous cup. If three lies were said over it, it would burst in pieces. But if three truths were said over it, it would reunite. Cormac learned that his family had been safe the whole time they had been missing, as guests of Manannan, King of the Land of Promise. Manannan gave him the cup in order to help Cormac with judgments involving truth and falsehood. Cormac also sees a pig that is set to boil in a cauldron: Manannan tells Cormac that it will not cook until a truth is told for each quarter of the pork. In turn, the guests around the table each tell a true tale about the wonders of the Celtic Otherworld; when the fourth tale is concluded, the pork is fit to be eaten.
SOUL-WISDOM Having had our material desires satisfied, we turn within to see what still needs accomplishing. Look for the opportunities that are unappreciated. Which falsehoods and burdens are weighing you down? Let them go in order to find fresh appetite for life.

5
COMBAT OF ART

DIVINATORY MEANING
UPRIGHT *Disappointment. Regret. Love, friendship, or alliances lost. Interior debate or struggle. Something is lost, but something is gained. Salvaging what one can from a situation. Inheritance after a death.*
REVERSED *Hopeful expectations. New alliances formed. Return of an old friend or partner. Reunion. Ancestry or kindred discovered. The end of a period of bereavement.*

BACKGROUND The brothers Amaethon and Gwydion fought "The Battle of the Trees" against Arawn, King of Annwfn (the Underworld). A white roebuck, a plover, and a greyhound pup escaped from Annwfn: Amaethon caught them and refused to give them back, so Arawn came after him. Gwydion made the trees fight on his side. Taliesin's poem *Cad Goddeu* tells of the muster of the trees:

> *I was at Caer Nefenhir,*
> *Where grass and trees came swiftly...*
> *Rush, you chiefs of the Wood...*
> *To hinder the hosts of the enemy.*

"The Battle of the Trees" became a byword in futility. The bardic significance of this battle is that each of the trees represents a letter of speech: this may have been a battle of bardic invective rather than a battle between Otherworldly forces.
SOUL-WISDOM Once we go on the offensive, we can damage or lose valuable relationships and friendships. What can be saved from your situation now?

6

FOUNDATION OF ART

DIVINATORY MEANING
UPRIGHT *Memories. Nostalgic remembrances or past vistas revisited. Childhood recollections bring comfort. Joys of home or homeland. Making a home. Childhood pleasures. Anniversaries.*
REVERSED *Atavism. Being stuck in the past. False comfort from outworn traditions. Memory of anniversaries brings pain. Outworn friendships. Future opportunities.*

BACKGROUND As students, the poets of Ireland were given subjects for compositions by their teachers. They then lay down in "the house of darkness" (a hut with no window or light) during the daytime, pursuing their metaphors in darkness and silence. In the evening, lights were brought in and they recited their poems from memory. Some later traditions speak of the students covering their eyes with their garments and keeping a large stone upon their bodies in order to help them stay awake. The poetic schools sat during the winter months when the days were shorter. Poems written around the time of the breakdown of the poetic academies in the mid-17th century speak of students bemoaning the call of the cuckoo because it heralded the end of their term of study. There are also many laments for the loss of "the house of memory," as well as poems that castigate the "modern" fashion of composition in the open air, in full daylight.

SOUL-WISDOM Wisdom and inspiration come best in moments of stillness and recollection. Instead of rushing on to the next activity, take time to commune with what is nurturing. What memories, dreams, and symbols give you life?

7

ADVENTURE OF ART

DIVINATORY MEANING

UPRIGHT *Illusions and fantasies. Daydreams. Escapist scenarios. Unrealistic attitudes or expectations. Wishful thinking. Self-deception. Dangerous indulgence of whims. Addiction to substances. Unhealthy dependence upon divination.*

REVERSED *Realization of deeply held desires or visions. Implementation or manifestation of dreams. Recognition of meaningful symbols or guiding archetypes within one's life. Resolutions upheld by the will.*

BACKGROUND The invading Fomorians carried off the Dagda's harper, Uaitne. Lugh, Dagda, and Ogma pursued the enemy until they came to the banqueting hall of King Bres of the Fomorians, where the harp was hanging on the wall. The Dagda had bound certain melodies into the harp that could only be activated by his call, so he cried out: "Come Oak of Two Greens, come Four-Angled music, come winter, come summer. Mouths of harps, bags, and pipes, come forth!" The harp came toward him of its own volition, killing nine men in the process. When it was in his hands, the Dagda played three melodies: the wail-strain, which made the company cry; the smile-strain, which made them laugh; and finally the sleep-strain, which put them to sleep – enabling the rescuers, harp, and harper to escape unhurt.

SOUL-WISDOM What we envisage or dream can manifest itself if we give it sufficient energy. However, using the Otherworldly powers for recreation or curiosity, without responsibility, can bring us into trouble. What is illusory and what is symbolically true here?

8
ELOPEMENT OF ART

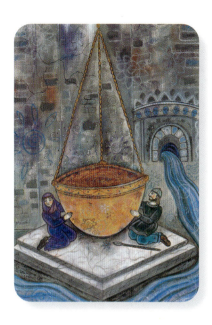

DIVINATORY MEANING
UPRIGHT *Abandonment of plans. Disenchantment with the run of your life. Emotional ambivalence. Turning away from a relationship. Retrenchment to re-establish priorities. Gain brings little joy.*
REVERSED *Success is attained. Great joy. Feasting or parties. A hectic social round.*

BACKGROUND While out hunting a white boar, Pryderi pursued it into a vast castle. On going into the castle, he found neither his dogs nor the boar, but only a fountain and, resting upon a marble slab and suspended by chains from the air, a beautiful golden bowl. Stretching out his hands, he found himself stuck to the bowl. When her son didn't come home, Rhiannon followed his tracks till she came to the castle and also stuck fast to the bowl. Only the cunning of her husband, Manawyddan, helped rescue them from their imprisonment. He discovered that this enchantment is caused by Llwyd ap Cil Coed, a cousin of Rhiannon's former suitor, Gwawl (see page 86). During their Otherworldly imprisonment, Rhiannon is ignominiously made to wear the hay-collar of an ass and Pryderi has to wear the door-striker of the gates about his neck.
SOUL-WISDOM Sometimes the issue before us loses focus or importance and we realize that it is not for us. Seeking a deeper understanding, we have to retire from the round of life and start afresh. Where are your energies uselessly committed?

9
REVELATION OF ART

DIVINATORY MEANING
UPRIGHT *The fulfillment of desire. Wishes granted. Physical wellbeing and comfort. Great satisfaction. Material abundance. Difficulties overthrown.*
REVERSED *Wishes prove elusive. Material loss. Self-satisfaction or complacency. Wasting opportunity by living in a totally material way. Mistakes. Misplaced expectations.*

BACKGROUND Conn of a Hundred Battles asked how many kings of his line would reign after him. No sooner had he asked, than he and his poet, Cesarn, found themselves in the Otherworld. They entered a great hall where the Goddess of Sovereignty sat in a crystal chair, crowned with a golden diadem. There was a silver vat with golden edges before her and a golden cup beside her. Also at her side sat the spiritual form of the God Lugh. The Goddess of Sovereignty gave Conn food and asked Lugh to whom the cup of red lordship (ale) should be poured. Lugh named every successor of Conn's in order, while Cesarn recorded these in ogam on staves of Yew. The Goddess of Sovereignty's duty is to defend the land and ensure that worthy candidates become rulers. By their unique relationship with her, kings like Conn (and Niall, see page 73) are married to the land and maintain that contract by faithful husbandry.

SOUL-WISDOM Wishes come true for those who keep the longing alive. Ensure that you really want what you wish for. Rescind any wishes that are no longer appropriate. What is your heart's true desire?

10
QUEST OF ART

DIVINATORY MEANING
UPRIGHT *Contentment. Lasting happiness. A peaceful heart and home. Tranquillity. Honor or reputation recognized. Joy. Harmonious order in the environment. Blessing.*
REVERSED *Discontentment. Unhappiness. A quarrelsome home life. Strife. Dishonor or betrayal. Criminal destruction. Wasteland.*

BACKGROUND The Well of Nine Hazels, also known as the Well of Segais, is the abode of the Salmon of Wisdom. It is mystically linked with the source of Boyne, which poets believed to be the wellspring of poetic inspiration. The Salmon of the Well imbibed the nuts that fell into the water from the nine Hazel trees. Whoever caught and ate the salmon would be imbued with its wisdom and filled with *imbas* or inspiration. The salmon was captured by Finn Eces, an elderly druid. His apprentice at the time was young Fionn mac Cumhail. Finn Eces asked Fionn to cook the salmon for him but, while it was cooking, some liquor from the salmon splashed out onto Fionn's thumb and it was he who gained the inspiration from the well. Subsequently, Fionn had only to put his thumb between his teeth and bite upon it to gain access to the wisdom of the well, in this Irish version of the source-of-all-knowledge story.
SOUL-WISDOM Fulfillment and lasting happiness rely upon our deep engagement with and respect for the causes of joy. How can you best share the blessing or gift you've received with those who can also respect them?

WOMAN OF ART

DIVINATORY MEANING
UPRIGHT *Someone who is loyal, helpful, and meditative; empathetic and understanding; artistic, and creative; intuitive, and sensitive. News of a birth. Creative visions. Help is available.*
REVERSED *Someone inclined to dabble in too many things. A dreamer or wastrel; too impressed by signs and wonders. Beware of being too naive. Wasted talents. News of deception.*

BACKGROUND Boann (Cow-Wealth) is the eponymous Goddess of the Boyne River. She had many partners, including Nechtan who jealously guarded the Well of Segais (see Quest of Art, page 93); he allowed no one else save he and his three cupbearers to go there. According to one tradition, Boann went secretly and walked around the well *tuathal* or widdershins (anticlockwise). This caused the waters of the well to rise up and inundate her, forming the Boyne River. But in a variant story, Boann's partner is Elcmar, Lord of the Bruig (modern-day Newgrange, in the Boyne Valley in Ireland). The Dagda slept with Boann while Elcmar was absent and, afterward, Boann gave birth to Oengus mac Og. Subsequently, Boann organized the quest for Oengus' dream-beloved, Caer Ibormeith.

SOUL-WISDOM The bounty of Boann nurtures our creative impulses and allows them to come to maturity through encouragement and devotion. Make sure that you give a generous amount of time to the development of your creative visions. Who or what supports your inner vision?

WARRIOR OF ART

DIVINATORY MEANING

UPRIGHT *A young man who is imaginative and aspiring; emotionally receptive, sensual, and charming. He is an artistic and visionary soul, a romantic dreamer. A proposition or invitation. Advancement or promotion.*
REVERSED *A deceptive escapist. A confidence-trickster. A narcissistic poseur; emotionally immature, passive, and irresponsible. Lies and fraudulent activity. Check all propositions very carefully.*

BACKGROUND Oengus mac Og was the love child of Boann and the Dagda. The Dagda desired Boann and sent her partner, Elcmar, away on service for a year, though it magically seemed no longer than a day to Elcmar. During that time Oengus was born. He was nicknamed "Mac Og" or "Son of Youth," because Boann remarked, "Young is the son who was begotten at daybreak and born between dawn and evening." Oengus' home became the sanctuary for the souls of famous lovers Diarmuid O'Duibhne and the transformed Etain. As a young man, Oengus dreamed of a beautiful maiden and became lovesick. A search discovered that the dream-woman was Caer Ibormeith (Yew-Berry) who lived as a swan every other year on the legendary Loch Bel Dragon. Oengus correctly identified Caer from her companion swans: he became a swan and they both took wing to celebrate their love. Oengus is shown with four birds flying about his head, representing his kisses.
SOUL-WISDOM Oengus is compassionate to all lovers. He offers a place of sanctuary where they can hide and a period of restfulness in which dreams can appear and be clarified. Who or what kindles your dreaming, romantic soul?

QUEEN OF ART

DIVINATORY MEANING

UPRIGHT *A visionary woman, able to implement her dreams. Emotionally mature, loving, sensitive to others' needs, she prefers home to the world at large, and is attuned to the resonances of music, poetry, and the arts as soul-food. She enjoys a contemplative and creative existence. Pleasure.*

REVERSED *A woman who is emotionally unbalanced and insecure. Worries about imagined problems. Escapes from reality. Paranoia, emotional dishonesty, or unreliability. Oversensitivity. Vulnerability.*

BACKGROUND Brighid (The High One) is the matron of healers, smiths, and poets (see also II The Guardian, page 26). The daughter of the Dagda, she married King Bres. Their son, Ruadan, was slain by the smith, Goibhniu, and Brighid then made the first keening that was ever heard in Ireland. Other traditions make Brighid the mother of Brian, Iuchair, and Iucharba, who met untimely deaths at the hands of Lugh. Brighid is frequently seen as an autonomous Goddess of Creative Wisdom, a mother and teacher of a spiritual lineage claimed by creative people. Her festival occurs on February 1st, or Imbolc. The Goddess Brighid and St. Brigit of Kildare share the same feast day and similar iconography, including the eternal flame of creativity.

SOUL-WISDOM Brighid is the mother of memory, able to call upon the resources of life to nourish, heal, and instruct. She keeps alive the sacred fires of creativity and kindles our creative flame. Who or what nurtures your soul?

KING OF ART

DIVINATORY MEANING
UPRIGHT *A creative and spiritual man, of deep emotional reserves. He is calm, with a clear sense of responsibility; compassionate, reliable, and generous. Someone of a philosophical, mystical, or religious background. Liberal attitudes. Kindness.*
REVERSED *A two-faced seducer; dishonest and shifty. Stealing honor or reputation. A violent neurotic. Sexual debauchery. Sarcasm or irony.*

BACKGROUND Like his British counterpart Lleu, Lugh had to win his own name, Lamfhota or "Long Hand." He is also known as "the Samildanach" or "many-gifted one," since he can perform all the arts and crafts. Lugh overthrew his tyrannical grandfather, Balor, by piercing Balor's magical single eye. He acceded to the leadership of the Tuatha de Danann and then slew his father's murderers. Lugh is said to have invented the board game of *fidhcell* and to have instituted horseracing at the festival that bears his name. This festival is Lughnasa, held on August 1st in honor of his foster mother, Tailtiu. Lugh championed Cuchulainn, and even took his place when the Ulster hero was fatigued. His bright, light-bestowing, and powerful attributes and some of his festivals became associated with those of St. Michael after Christianization. Like Odin, a raven is one of Lugh's personas.

SOUL-WISDOM Lugh's far-flung spear covers great distances, while his light clears away darkness and obstruction. By drawing upon the creative heart within us, we find the inner confidence and calm to withstand troubles. What does your generous impulse bid you do now?

Suit of Knowledge

LUGHNASA *The Season of Fall*

1
AUGURY OF KNOWLEDGE

DIVINATORY MEANING
UPRIGHT *Knowledge. Prosperity. Wealth. Ecstasy. Sovereignty. Treasure. Spiritual riches. The touchstone of self-realization. Recognition and inauguration.*
REVERSED *Ignorance. Wealth misused. Corruption. Miserliness. Greed. Inability or refusal to understand cause and effect. Being overlooked in promotion.*

BACKGROUND The Lia Fail, or Stone of Fal, came from the Otherworldly city of Falias and would cry out for the rightful sovereign. Falias, the place of Knowledge, was guarded by the poet Morfessa (the Wise One). Many sacred sites and monuments have their guardian spirit, who acts as an oracular mouth for the special qualities of that place. The augury or prophecy given by the Stone of Fal is received by all living beings through their individual relationship with the earth and with their own particular home, country, and environment that nourishes them. The spirit of the suit of Knowledge is most clearly understood through the element of earth, from the many-omened movements of the middle realm and in the season of fall.

SOUL-WISDOM Morfessa imparts potent knowledge of the earth's wisdom to every cell of our bodies. The ancestral bequest of our blood lineage and the acclaim of our spiritual kindred – those who are companions upon our soul's quest – create a unique wealth in each of us. What are you being called upon to use from your innate spiritual treasury?

2
DIALOGUE OF KNOWLEDGE

DIVINATORY MEANING
UPRIGHT *Flexibility. The daring to launch audacious new ventures that may not necessarily succeed. Living by one's wits. Playing ball with life. Lightheartedness.*
REVERSED *Embarrassment. Lack of confidence. Fear of failure. Caution. Too many commitments. Biting off more than one can chew. Enforced gaiety.*

BACKGROUND When the young Irish poet Nede hears of his father's death, he returns home to take up his claim to his father's chair of poetry. Making himself a beard of straw to simulate maturity, he goes to sit in the chair when he is challenged by the older poet Ferchertne. They then have a long dialogue in which each demonstrates his poetic skill to the other. Finally, Nede realizes that his expectations have been full of pride and he humbly admits his opponent's superior skill. However, Ferchertne was merely testing young Nede's qualification to take his father's place and, appointing himself as his patron, he formally seats Nede in the chair and affirms his role.

SOUL-WISDOM The ability to adapt and not become static is a great gift. How is your current strategy being challenged? What needs to change or to be handled in a more playful way?

3
COURTSHIP OF KNOWLEDGE

DIVINATORY MEANING
UPRIGHT *Mastery in work. Perfection. Professional dignity or renown. Educational prowess. Exceptional competence in one's chosen field. Awards, degrees, or certification. Faithfulness to high values.*
REVERSED *Mediocrity. Lack of skill. Commonplace values. Average abilities. Preoccupation with gain rather than serving value. Adequately done work.*

BACKGROUND When the invading Milesians try to conquer Ireland and seize it from the Tuatha de Danann people, they initially find themselves defeated. The Milesian poet Amairgin takes radical action by applying directly to the spirits of the land for their support. He visits the Goddesses of Ireland – Banba, Fotla, and Eriu – in turn. He promises each one that the Milesians will name Ireland after the Goddess in question, in return for her support. Having made a three-way promise, Amairgin approaches Ireland with his people and sings an incantation of welcome to the land, and the Milesians are successful in the invasion. The land of Ireland is still known as Eriu or Eire.

SOUL-WISDOM By striving to produce our best work in accordance with our highest ideals, we honor the gifts and abilities with which we are innately gifted. In what ways are you being asked to produce your best effort in this situation?

4
JUDGMENT OF KNOWLEDGE

DIVINATORY MEANING
UPRIGHT *Stable power. Love of material wealth or possessions. Financial security. Possessiveness. Economic control. Lack of generosity. Hoarding. Gifts unused. Talents unpracticed.*
REVERSED *Disorder. Financial setbacks or loss of possessions. Carelessness with money. Spendthrift. Suspense or delay. Profligate with one's gifts or talents.*

BACKGROUND In the Welsh story, the youth Gilfaethwy is hopelessly in love with Goewin, the virgin footholder of his uncle, Math. Gilfaethwy's brother, Gwydion, causes Math to go to war, thereby separating Math from Goewin long enough for Gilfaethwy to rape her. Math's judgment is that he himself will marry Goewin to restore her good name, while the wrongdoing brothers shall both be turned into animals for three years. Gilfaethwy becomes, in turn, a hind, a boar, and a bitch wolf, while Gwydion becomes a stag, a sow, and a wolf. Each year the shapechanged brothers mate with each other and produce young. At the end of their punishment, Math turns the brothers back into human form and adopts their offspring as his own.
SOUL-WISDOM When we yearn possessively after another's wealth or good fortune, we disrespect our own gifts and potential, and violate the fabric of life. Learning to value what we have and to respect who we really are upholds the stability of our community. What is being hoarded or coveted here?

5
COMBAT OF KNOWLEDGE

DIVINATORY MEANING
UPRIGHT *Trouble. Misfortune. Exclusion. Destitution. Loss of home. Loneliness. Loss of job. Meaninglessness. Impoverishment. Failure. Loss of faith. Bare survival.*
REVERSED *Improvement. Charity. Help is offered. Parttime work. New affinities and friendships in adversity. Fresh meaning is discovered. Faith is restored.*

BACKGROUND The Otherworldly Macha married Crunnchu mac Agnoman but warned him not to mention her name or she would be lost to him. Crunnchu agreed, but at a gathering where people were praising the speed of the king's horses, he boasted that his wife was an even faster runner. The king sent for Macha to prove the assertion. She asked to be excused because she was pregnant, but the king would not allow any delay. Macha warned him, "Then the shame that is upon you will be greater than that upon me, and a heavier punishment upon you." She then outran the horses but, at the finishing post, gave birth to twins. At her birth pangs, everyone present experienced a similar weakness. Macha then pronounced her curse: that until the ninth generation the men of Ulster would experience the weakness of a woman in child-bed for five nights and four days when their enemies were closing upon them. This story gave the name to the place Emain Macha (The Twins of Macha), just outside modern-day Armagh in Northern Ireland.

SOUL-WISDOM Our troubles are often seeded by our own actions and attitudes. What issues of respect and trust are being excluded here?

6
FOUNDATION OF KNOWLEDGE

DIVINATORY MEANING
UPRIGHT *Inherited wisdom. Benevolence. Generosity. Sharing knowledge. Gifts. Acts of kindness. Benefits, rewards, and dividends. Service to the community or commonwealth. Blessing.*
REVERSED *Cultural jealousy. Envy. Parsimony. Being unable to receive. Acts of selfishness that endanger community. Being shortchanged in expected payments.*

BACKGROUND The druidic tradition of Britain was disrupted and outlawed at the coming of the second Roman invasion in the first century C.E., but it continued in Ireland until beyond the coming of Christianity in the fifth century. Druids were the counselors, philosophers, diviners, shamans, and spiritual mediators of the Celtic world but, above all, they were the keepers of the sacred wisdom. The tradition of druids meeting in groves or *nemetons* is well established and, although stone circles were built in an earlier megalithic era, it is very likely that druids also utilized these sacred sites and understood their lore and alignment with celestial phenomena. According to druidic tradition, those who maintain "the perpetual choirs of song," the guardianship of the tribe's integrity, sustain the blessed harmony of the land.

SOUL-WISDOM The blessing that we can each bestow upon our community is often locked up in us because we feel separate from it. Every act of generous service to the community in which we live becomes a blessing that radiates to the whole world. What needs to be shared in this situation?

7

ADVENTURE OF KNOWLEDGE

DIVINATORY MEANING
UPRIGHT *Hard work. The rigors of study. Career treadmill. Results slow to arrive. Success delayed. Dissatisfaction with a long-term project. Speculation.*
REVERSED *Uneasiness about work. Fruitless study. Work and financial rewards cancel each other out: no advancement. Loans, debts, and financial worries. Poor investments.*

BACKGROUND One Samhain eve, the night when ghosts and spirits walk abroad, King Ailill and Maeve of Connacht offered a prize to anyone brave enough to go outside and slip a rope around the corpse on the gallows outside. This dare was taken up by one man only, Nera. As soon as he approached the body, Nera had a vision of the hill-fort of Cruachan burning. He was transported to a hill of the *sidhe* (the Otherworldly abode of the Faery) where he married a *bansidhe* (banshee); she told him that his vision had not yet happened and was preventable. She gave him a spray of summer fruit to take back with him, and made him promise to return to rescue her and her child. Nera then went back to warn Ailill that the Faery meant to burn Cruachan, then he disappeared into the land of Faery and was never seen again.

SOUL-WISDOM When work is dull, we are often tempted to take risks or to introduce the spice of change. Speculation may bring temporary excitement but nothing can displace hard work. When patience and efforts wear thin, return to the source of your inspiration. What continued effort is needed here?

8
ELOPEMENT OF KNOWLEDGE

DIVINATORY MEANING

UPRIGHT *Study or apprenticeship. Practical application to a task. Engagement or absorption in work. Commissions. Craftsmanship. Proficiency or qualification in a technique.*
REVERSED *False assumption of proficiency. Vanity and conceit replace application to task. Taking short cuts to achieve quick results. Forgery or plagiarism.*

BACKGROUND The Welsh Goddess Ceridwen's cauldron of wisdom was set to brew for a year and a day in order to give her ugly son, Afagddu, the attributes of knowledge. However, she set the boy Gwion to tend the cauldron and, when the brew boiled over, he caught some drops from the cauldron on his fingers. When he thrust his fingers into his mouth to cool the burns, he accidentally imbibed all knowledge and immediately realized that Ceridwen would soon be after him. He turned into a hare and ran away, but Ceridwen followed as a greyhound. He became a fish, and she an otter. He became a bird, and she a hawk. Finally, he dived into a pile of wheat, and she turned herself into a red hen and scrabbled him up into her crop. Nine months later, he was born as the great poet Taliesin.
SOUL-WISDOM For us to attain any mastery in any area of learning, we have to engage and connect with the knowledge already within us. This takes a period of assimilation and practice. What needs to be assimilated?

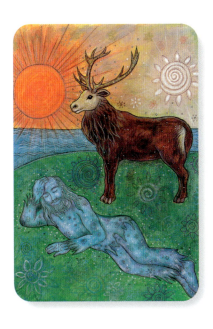

9
REVELATION OF KNOWLEDGE

DIVINATORY MEANING
UPRIGHT *Accomplishment. Practical wisdom. Recognition and acknowledgment, especially after lone work. Discretion. Attainment through conscientious endeavor. The rewards of labor. Independence. Love of nature. Mature self-image.*
REVERSED *Dissipation of gains. Paranoia arising from too much solitude. Lack of discipline. Projects quickly abandoned. Faltering self-reliance.*

BACKGROUND Tuan mac Carill was the sole survivor of the first invaders to reach Ireland. He grew older and older until finally he began to feel a change come upon him. He then shapechanged into different life forms, witnessing each subsequent invasion of Ireland. As a stag, he saw the arrival of the people of Nemed. Outliving the Nemedians, he became a wild boar and witnessed the invasion of the Fir Bolg. Then he changed into the form of a hawk, seeing the invasion of the Tuatha de Danann and the Milesians. With each transformation, he experienced a new lease of life. Finally, he took the form of a salmon, until he was caught by a fisherman and served up as a dish for the queen of King Cairell. As the queen ate the fish, the soul of Tuan passed into her womb. The child was named Tuan, who remembered everything from each of his existences.
SOUL-WISDOM After working alone without reward or recognition, it is good to receive reward and the acknowledgment of others. Knowledge deepens in solitary endeavor. What is your gut feeling, your deepest knowledge about this matter?

10
QUEST OF KNOWLEDGE

DIVINATORY MEANING

UPRIGHT *Ancestral wisdom. Enjoyment of blessings. Safety. Security of home and possessions. Inheritances, family matters, blood relations, and spiritual kindred. Valuable incorporation into institutions. Archives available.*
REVERSED *Ancestral expectations hold sway. Failure to respect tradition. Gambling away family inheritance. Squandering cultural or spiritual treasures. Burdensome care of elderly relatives or administration of family affairs. Superstitious observance.*

BACKGROUND The Cauldron of Annwfn, in the British Underworld, is the object of Arthur's quest. He goes to Annwfn upon his ship, Prydwen, along with three companies of men, in an attempt to steal the Cauldron. The Cauldron is attended by nine sisters, in whose keeping are the gifts of knowledge. The Cauldron's special property is that it will not boil food for cowards, and therefore only the most select and worthy guests can sit down to eat from it. From that raid, only seven returned, including Arthur and his poet, Taliesin, who recorded their exploits. The ninth-century poem is one of the earliest literary pairings of Arthur and the Cauldron, which is the earliest correlative of the Grail.
SOUL-WISDOM Find the freedom and blessings of tradition and avoid becoming institutionalized. Every generation needs guardians of wisdom to rekindle the handed down traditions. What is the received wisdom on this matter? What solutions can you offer yourself?

WOMAN OF KNOWLEDGE

DIVINATORY MEANING
UPRIGHT *A young person who is careful, practical, and patient; studious, learned, and reflective; responsible, conformist, and persistent. Concentration. Good management. Care. News of money.*
REVERSED *Someone who is rebellious, extravagant, and dissipated. Failure to learn from mistakes. Inability to face the facts. Wastefulness. News of money lost.*

BACKGROUND Airmid, whose name means "Measure of Grain", was the daughter of Diancecht, the physician of the Tuatha de Danann. She assisted her brother, Miach, in replacing the hand of King Nuadu when it was severed in battle. But Diancecht was so jealous of Miach's success that he slew his own son. From the joints of Miach's dead body grew 365 herbs to assist with healing. Airmid sorted them into their different kinds of healing qualities, but her father muddled them up again. It is said that only those graced by spiritual knowledge can know the herbs' particular qualities. Airmid also helped sing healing spells over the Well of Slane (or Health). When the Tuatha de Danann brought their dead to this well, the waters miraculously revived them again.
SOUL-WISDOM Airmid's patience brings muddle into a state of order. Her healing voice and wisdom are heard in the friends who accompany our soul's track. Who or what is offering you good advice here?

WARRIOR OF KNOWLEDGE

DIVINATORY MEANING

UPRIGHT *A man who is responsible, uncomplaining, and hard-working; reliable, serviceable, and trustworthy. Conservative and cautious, he works in an orderly and routine way. Loyalty. Job prospects or financial matters in the air.*

REVERSED *Someone who is directionless or stuck in a rut. Timidity, stagnation, and dullness. Idleness or, at the other extreme, workaholism. Carelessness. Irresponsibility. Inability to grow or to stretch abilities.*

BACKGROUND Mabon has been lost since the beginning of time, stolen from the side of his mother, Modron, when he was only three nights old. He is rediscovered when the youth Culhwch falls in love with Olwen, daughter of the giant Yspaddaden. The giant sets Culhwch many impossible tasks, chief of which is to steal a razor, comb, and scissors from between the ears of a monstrous boar that ravages the countryside of Britain. Only Mabon can achieve this task. With the help of the most ancient animals, Mabon is freed from imprisonment. He wins the razor, comb, and scissors that will shave Yspaddaden's hair and beard for his daughter's wedding to Culhwch (see also Quest of Skill, page 78). Mabon is derived from the earlier Celtic deity Maponos, who is related to Apollo.

SOUL-WISDOM In his liberated form, Mabon enables the accomplishment of slow tasks that take organic lengths of time, and bestows patience and conscientious attention to detail. Only by such attention can we eventually achieve things with speed and exactitude. Who or what can be trusted in this situation?

QUEEN OF KNOWLEDGE

DIVINATORY MEANING
UPRIGHT *A woman of dignity, grace, and generosity. Prosperity. Enjoyment of luxury. Security and stability. Steadfastness in achieving goals. Improving one's environment. Good organization.*
REVERSED *Someone who is mistrustful and suspicious or, at the other extreme, someone who relies too much on others. Melancholia, moroseness, or moodiness. A disordered home environment. Fear of failure. Lack of self-confidence.*

BACKGROUND Danu, Ana, or Dôn is the ancestress and Great Goddess of the Celtic peoples. The root of her name, meaning "wealth or abundance," is found in numerous rivers from India to Ireland. She is the grandmother of Ecne (the personification of knowledge) and the progenitor of the Tuatha de Danann or "the Family of Danu." In Munster, Ireland, the twin hills of Dá Cioch Anann or "the Paps of Anu" are named after her. In British tradition she is called Dôn, where she is the sister of Math and the mother of Arianrhod, Gwydion, Gilfaethwy, Gofannon, and Amaethon. Her husband is Beli Mawr. In Wales, "Llys Dôn" or "the Court of Don" is the name given to the constellation Cassiopaea. Danu's attributes became attached to those of St. Anne, who occupies the unique position of God's grandmother.
SOUL-WISDOM Danu/Dôn weaves the lineages and fates of her children on her starry loom, bestowing her wealth upon those able to receive. She shows us how to value our inherited gifts while not becoming tangled up in ancestral bequests and expectations. Who or what is being woven into this situation?

KING OF KNOWLEDGE

DIVINATORY MEANING
UPRIGHT *A man who is practical, traditional, and well-off; successful, experienced, and unadventurous; resourceful and pragmatic. He understands money and the material world. Wise investments. Respect for the past and the family.*
REVERSED *Someone who is dogmatic and stupid; stubborn and impractical. A cheapskate, easily corrupted. Danger. Vice. The end justifies the means.*

BACKGROUND The Dagda or "Good God" is the leader of the Tuatha de Danann by reason of his all-round accomplishments as warrior, king, craftsman, and enchanter (see also I The Decider, page 25). He also assumes the shape of an earthy peasant, in a tunic that shows his rump. He possessed the Cauldron that came from Muirias (see Augury of Art, page 84) from which no one ever went unsatisfied. His great club was so huge that it had to be dragged on wheels behind him, leaving deep ruts in his wake; this is also a reference to his virility with many women. He trysts with the Morrigan while she squats over a river and is the father of Midir and other kings of the Faery hills. He had two magical pigs: one was always alive, while the other was always being cooked.

SOUL-WISDOM If we want to access the riches of knowledge or wealth, the Dagda will help us activate our own deep potential so that we can become the people we really are, rather than the ones we think we are. What is the essential wisdom in this situation?

THE BRIGHT KNOWLEDGE

"What is your name?" asked Medb of the maiden.

"I am Fedelm, poetess of Connacht," she replied.

"Whence do you come?" asked Medb.

"From Albion after learning the art of divination," said Fedelm.

"Have you the power of prophecy called imbas forosna?"

"I have indeed," replied Fedelm.

TÁIN BÓ CUAILNGE
(translation: Caitlín Matthews)

IV

Divining our Destiny

The root meaning of the word "divination" is "asking the gods or spirits." Celtic seers called upon the spirits of nature, the four elements, ancestors, and deities to help show them the way.

Divination can help open and clear the way to our destiny. In Celtic tradition, the Gifting Mothers of the cauldron imbue each soul with its gifts and talents: our part is to find and use those gifts. Divining our destiny means coming into focus with our essence and attuning to the spirits and influences with which we have kindred connection.

Destiny is not a dogmatic set of predestined rules, but is more like discovering the rhythm of the music and moving accordingly. When we find our own coordinates, we come into harmony with the web of the worlds and heal the imbalances of our lives. We become attuned to the universe and are in tune with our authentic selves.

By cross-correlating the given or known coordinates with the unseen or yet unrealized ones, the tarot reader can look between the worlds and see the reflection of our actions, observing which actions seem to unbalance life and which ones bring it into harmony again.

Each tarot reading is like consulting the map of the soul's landscape, which helps correlate our progress and give insights into where we are right now. Tarot is not a divinity that dictates how we are to proceed. Our own attitudes, motivations, understandings, and freewill are the factors that determine how we will walk through that landscape.

Quests and Questions

Our soul's journey is a quest upon which we are each engaged. Quests do not reveal themselves right away, they unfold sequentially. The way in which questers keep themselves on track is to keep asking: where am I going? who am I? what help is available? how do I keep going? when am I going to rest? There are cardinal rules about divination that concern the question. The first is: if you don't want to know the answer, don't ask the question. And the second is: ask the right question. Always have a good question or issue to ask the cards – time spent on defining the issue is time well spent. The clearer your question, the more you can learn about divination.

GUIDELINES FOR FRAMING QUESTIONS

1 What is the issue about? Get the central subject of the question clear and keep your question short and to the point.
2 What is the need underlying it? Is this question really necessary? If it moves you and the issue is fouling up your life, then it's the right question.
3 Does something need to be considered or acted on before this question is asked? Prioritize your needs and take the one at the top of the heap.
4 Does the issue involve another person? Be ethical about asking questions about others. Try to frame the question so that your needs and issues are emphasized, rather than the other person's.
5 Is the issue framed in a positive rather than a negative way? For example, instead of asking "Why don't I succeed?" ask instead "Show me how to succeed."
6 Does your question rest on an unproven assumption? Asking "How shall I spend my lottery winnings?" assumes a great deal if you haven't yet bought the ticket!

7 Is your question conditional upon something or someone else? Asking "Should I attend the party?" would be better reframed as "What are the consequences of attending the party?" Avoid conditional questions and make some personal decisions to help motivate your question.
8 Is there a choice involved in your question? In issues about choice, do a reading on each of the choices. Avoid "either/or" questions such as "Will I go to Paris or Biarritz this year?"
9 Is there space for Spirit in your question? Asking "How can I heal the earth?" is not only presumptuous, it encloses the answer within the narrow possibilities of your own limits: to open the issue to wider influence, it might be rephrased as "How can the earth be healed?" When your question is well focused, shuffle or mix the cards while you consider your question. You will know when to stop when you get a sense of going around again. If you are reading for someone else, do not shuffle the cards. The person for whom the reading is intended should shuffle the cards while considering his or her question.

The Three Illuminations Spread

This spread is especially good when the issue is clouded or the client is too confused to take appropriate action. The spread is based upon an Irish triad that speaks of the three candles that illumine every darkness: truth, nature, and knowledge. Cards 1–4 show the basis of the issue that is in darkness. Cards 5–7 show the three candles that illuminate the issue.

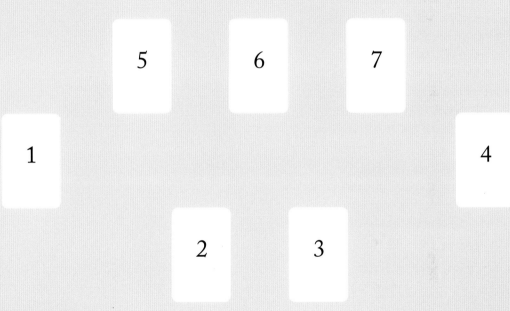

1 The basis of the issue
2 Your hopes
3 Your fears
4 The kind of action that will enable the outcome
5 The truth about the issue
6 The innate nature of the issue
7 The hidden knowledge about the issue

This spread can be very helpful on those occasions when a situation is complex or the client is confused. The Three Illuminations Spread will cast a clear shaft of light on the matter.

Soul-Protectors Spread

This short spread is a useful daily reading to use when you are learning the cards. It acts as an augury or prophecy of elements that surround your day. You can either draw cards the night before for the next day, or you can draw them early in the morning and look out for their influence and help throughout the day.

    This spread is based upon the Celtic understanding of the directions. That which lies ahead or in the east is our forerunner and path-clearer; that which lies behind has motivated us. What lies on our left hand is challenging. what lies on our right hand is friendly; Beneath us is that which empowers us; above us lies whatever inspires us. In the still center is our own soul. We come to a better sense of orientation on our way by identifying, meeting, and working closely with the allies of the spiritual directions.

Shuffle the cards, asking "Who are my Soul Protectors for today?"

1 AHEAD   Who/what opens the way for me today?
2 BEHIND   Who/what motivates me?
3 LEFT   Who/what challenges me?
4 RIGHT   Who/what supports me?
5 BENEATH   Who/what empowers me?
6 ABOVE   Who/what inspires me?
7 WITHIN   Who/what accompanies my soul today?

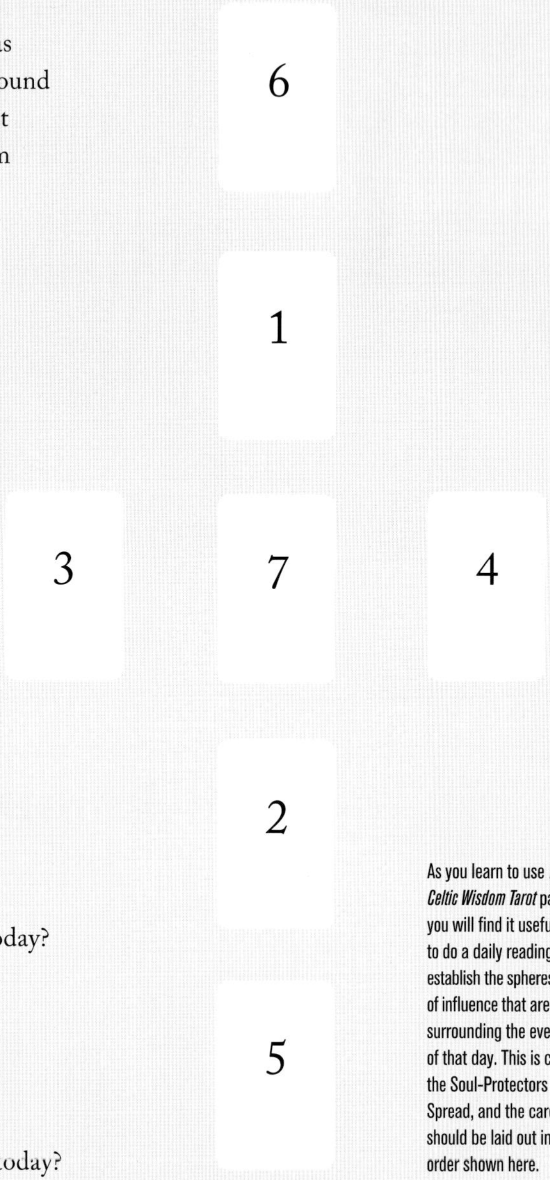

As you learn to use *The Celtic Wisdom Tarot* pack, you will find it useful to do a daily reading to establish the spheres of influence that are surrounding the events of that day. This is called the Soul-Protectors Spread, and the cards should be laid out in the order shown here.

Sample Soul-Protectors Spread

I drew these cards on the day that I attempted to get back down to work after a particularly difficult period of domestic disruption and family bereavement. So many reversed cards were very daunting but I nevertheless proceeded.

1. Dialogue of Knowledge (*reversed*) showed that the way ahead was blocked by too many commitments; I was attempting too much, too soon.
2. Warrior of Art (*reversed*) showed that I was unable to motivate myself because I was unable to take much responsibility: I felt like escaping from daily life and hiding away.
3. Woman of Knowledge (*reversed*) said the biggest challenge was the perceived waste of time caused by the disruptive last few weeks: part of me wanted to catch up, but the wiser part wanted to get away from things.
4. Woman of Skill (*reversed*) was a good friend to me, saying I needed to follow my own impulses: resistance to work wasn't something I should feel guilty about.
5. King of Skill (*reversed*) reinforced this message, showing me that empowerment was about having my own way today, as long as I was aware of the dangers of going to excess.
6. X The Spinner bade me look at the bigger picture of my life: a new cycle of energy was on its way and I could pick up on the correct wind, phase, and current.
7. VI The Lover said to look at my heart's desire: far better than trying to work today, was to do whatever I wanted, and not get tied up in coils of guilt about time wasted.

During a very difficult time, the author drew the seven cards shown here, and laid them out in the order shown opposite. The cards accurately reflected her situation, provided realistic ways of resolving the issues, and offered hope of better times to come.

The Five Streams of the Senses Spread

This reading draws upon the Otherworldly fountain of inspiration from which five streams ray out, each representing one of the senses we use to understand the world. Use this spread when you need to be really perceptive or to clarify a situation in which coordinates don't seem to match up. Read the cards in pairs (1+6, 2+7, 3+8, 4+9, 5+10) in order to see the conflict, lack of alignment or real attunement.
Cards 1–5 represent the situation as it appears on the surface
Cards 6–10 represent the hidden correlatives of the situation.

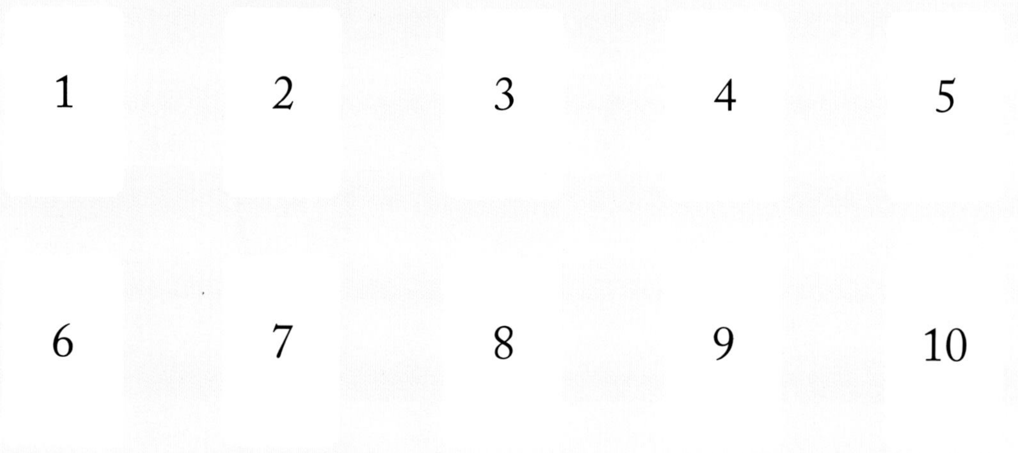

1   2   3   4   5

6   7   8   9   10

1 Sight: how does it appear?
2 Sound: how does it sound?
3 Taste: what is the flavor?
4 Feeling: how does it feel?
5 Smell: how does it smell?
6 Inner vision: what does this really look like?
7 Resonance: what is truly being communicated here?
8 Discrimination: what needs to be included/excluded?
9 Empathy: how am I in/out of accord with the situation?
10 Instinct: what is my gut reaction?

Lay out the cards in the order shown here, then read them in pairs from left to right: 1+6; 2+7; 3+8; 4+9; 5+10. This will reveal the difference between what is on the surface (cards 1–5) and what underlies appearances (cards 6–10).

The Co-Walkers Spread

In Scots Gaelic tradition, the *co-imuimeadh* or "co-walker" is the spiritual ally who literally "walks with" our soul. We often have questions about relationships between lovers, friends, family members, and work colleagues, as well as about our relationships with ancestors, spiritual allies, and associations. Draw extra cards to clarify any positions that are difficult to comprehend.

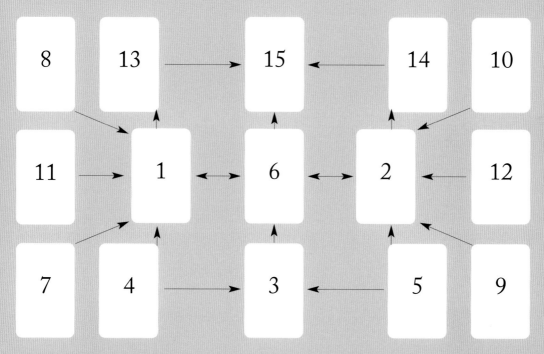

1 You now
2 Your partner/friend/associate now
3 How your relationship began
4 You then
5 Your partner then
6 Basis of your relationship now
7 Your needs
8 Your expectations
9 Your partner's needs
10 Your partner's expectations
11 What your partner has given you
12 What you have given your partner
13 Changes you must make
14 Changes your partner must make
15 Where your relationship is going

The Weaver's Celtic Cross Spread

This general spread physically interweaves the edges of the cards to create a real Celtic Cross. The cards are laid, facedown, as shown in figure 1 here; you will notice which ones are reversed from their backs. When you've interwoven the cards together to form a cross, slide one hand under the spread and, with your other hand steadying the top side, flip the cross over so that all the cards are face upward, as in figure 2.

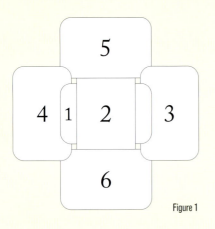

Figure 1

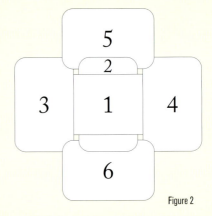

Figure 2

1 Yourself now
2 Basis of the situation
3 That which hinders or challenges
4 That which helps or supports
5 Overriding consideration/new focus
6 Old focus/unconscious preoccupation

If you want to explore the reading further, you can examine the nature of the hindrance, help, new focus, or preoccupation by laying down a new cross on any or all of card numbers 3, 4, 5, and 6, using the card you're exploring as an arm of the new cross. You can create a total of five interconnected crosses with this method. When you do this, the reading positions change the card that you've built out from and reveal significant information.

A new cross can be built from card 5 here. Augury of Skill will occupy a new position on the new cross: it will become card number 6, the bottom arm of the new cross.

A new cross can be built from card 3 here. The Empowerer will occupy a new position on the new cross: it will become card number 4, the right-hand arm of the new cross.

A new cross can be built from card 4 here. Courtship of Knowledge will occupy a new position on the new cross: it will become card number 3, the left-hand arm of the new cross.

A new cross can be built from card 6 here. Judgment of Skill will occupy a new position on the new cross: it will become card number 5, the top arm of the new cross.

The Seven Candles of Life Spread

This advanced but rewarding spread uses only the Wisdom Cards. It reveals hidden patterns and opportunities for major life issues and is useful for a good overview of things. The positions of this spread derive from the original sequence and layout of the Wisdom Cards.

This spread reveals The Seven Candles of Life: Will, Truth, Growth, Harmony, Lore, Devotion, and Energy; the cards can be read vertically as well as horizontally (see page 126). The chosen card here is VI The Lover to reflect the client's wish to ask about a new lover in this spread.

WILL	TRUTH	GROWTH	HARMONY	LORE	DEVOTION	ENERGY
1	2	3	4	5	6	7
8	9	10	11	12	13	14
15	16	17	18	19	20	21

Let's take an example. Suppose the recent death of someone has caused a big shift in your life and you need to reorient your focus, but can't see how. You might choose the card of the Liberator to create a story about how Death has rejigged your own life story. If your issue was about a new lover, you could choose the Lover; if it was about dreams and creative hopes for the future, you could choose the Dreamer card. Whatever your focus, this card now serves as the basis for a new story, and it is laid on the position 0, the Soul. Now shuffle the rest of the Wisdom Cards and lay them in sequence in the positions 1–21. The spread now reveals the story or unfolding journey of that issue.

Cards 1–7 on the top line reveal the conscious level – the basic issues as they appear in your life right now.

Cards 8–14 on the middle line reveal the unconscious level – the personal and possibly hidden agendas and understandings about the issue of which you are unaware.

Cards 15–21 on the bottom line reveal the superconscious level – the way in which the story can manifest itself through our attunement and practice.

Read the cards according to the position they occupy (the original Wisdom Card sequence) and their own specific meaning. You create your reading by continuing the sentences begun here.

0   This story is about . . .
1   The pattern of this matter is based upon . . .
2   The truth of the matter is shown by . . .
3   The nurture/lack of support has been through . . .
4   My autonomy has been challenged by . . .
5   My expectations have been changed by . . .
6   My desires have been committed to . . .
7   I find myself here at . . .
8   The deep resources I reach for are . . .
9   The truth that I need to confront is . . .

10 The hidden patterns are revealed by . . .
11 My integrity is invested in . . .
12 I am initiated by . . .
13 I am liberated by . . .
14 The assimilation I seek is by means of . . .
15 I can be free of fear when I . . .
16 I can be transformed when I allow the change of . . .
17 I can access my inspiration when I . . .
18 I can attune to my powers when I . . .
19 I can access wholeness when I . . .
20 I can renew my life by means of . . .
21 I can be my authentic self when I . . .

Finally, look vertically down the reading and read the three cards under each of the Seven Candles of Life to get a sense of the internal pattern of the reading. Which candle is burning most powerfully? Which candle is shedding least light?

Will: what caused this.
Truth: your understanding of this.
Growth: what you've passed through.
Harmony: the test or assimilation.
Lore: how you experience this situation.
Devotion: your commitment.
Energy: your action or the result.

Reading for Others

When we read for others, we encounter someone else's needs, hopes, and expectations. We also run into assumptions about divination that need to be addressed at the outset. Explain that tarot isn't magic, that the diviner isn't psychic, that the cards in any spread simply reveal ways through and over problems and are not fated, fixed coordinates of doomful prospect.

GUIDELINES FOR READING FOR OTHERS

1. Ensure that the location is suitable for undisturbed readings.
2. Discuss the issue and help the client to word the question (see pages 115–6).
3. Ask the client to look through the deck and choose any card to represent his- or herself in the current situation. This card is the significator and isn't shuffled back into the main deck. It becomes the witness of the reading.
4. Let the client shuffle the deck in silence, while asking the cards the question. Then take the shuffled deck and lay out the sequence of the chosen spread.
5. Let the reading unfold like a story: to help the client see the reading as a story or scenario, "walk" the significator card the client chose through the sequence of the reading. For example, you might start with "here you are at the beginning of this story, struggling with overwhelming demands" if Quest of Skill was drawn, and so on.
6. If you don't understand something in a reading, say so and move on to the next card, returning to it later. Invite the client to take one or more cards from the unused deck to augment the reading and read the troublesome card in relation to these.
7. Invite questions and input from the client. Reinforce with common sense and practical advice, and avoid negative predictions; respect the client's opinions.
8. Conclude by asking the client to formulate what he or she understands from the reading. When there's nothing left to discuss, finish cleanly, without lingering.

Interpretation

Interpretation is a very personal skill that develops over the years. Initially, it is customary to read the written meaning given in the book but, as your confidence grows, you will note significant symbols and correlatives in the cards and cross-relate them, making a story that has meaning. With greater experience, the cards seem to read themselves in relation to the question asked and the client sitting next to you. The better you know your pack, the more sophisticated your interpretation will become.

Read the cards according to their own meaning, their position in the reading, and their correlation to each other. Let the reading unfold like a story you are telling. If certain features of the cards leap out at you with more prominence, then mention them and weave them into the structure of your interpretation.

If you are having difficulty reading any card in your spread, refer to the Soul-Wisdom sections of the relevant cards and try to answer the questions posed there as truthfully as possible: this may help reveal something else about the cards in their particular positions. The questions to ask for each card are also summarized for easy reference on pages 130–131.

Sometimes "negative" cards appear on "positive" positions or vice versa; this is often a sign that the person is not considering the other side of his or her options. Look again at the question and see what wisdom lies hidden there. Also, look more closely at the predominant patterns the cards reveal when you've told the main story of the reading:

PREDOMINANCE OF WISDOM CARDS Momentous events are abroad. The soul-path is revealing itself dynamically.

PREDOMINANCE OF STORY CARDS The client is involved in his or her own everyday story and is less susceptible to the coordinates of the soul-path at this moment in time.

XI THE BALANCER

VIII THE EMPOWERER

XV THE CHALLENGER

A predominance of Wisdom Cards in a spread means that important events are taking place in the client's life.

PREDOMINANCE OF COURT CARDS May indicate other people involved in the issue or aspects of the client, especially if the question is about his or her personal change or growth.

PREDOMINANCE OF BATTLE CARDS Contention, difficulty, or decision.

PREDOMINANCE OF SKILL CARDS Enterprize, occupation, or abilities.

PREDOMINANCE OF ART CARDS Emotions, dreams, visions.

PREDOMINANCE OF KNOWLEDGE CARDS Lifestyle, work, physical or spiritual wealth.

PREDOMINANCE OF CARDS OF THE SAME NUMBER (Auguries, Dialogues, Courtships, and so on, see pages 49–50). Three or four similarly numbered cards may show which phase of the soul-path the client is currently working through.

REVERSED CARDS Either the client is upset or the question is of a distressing nature. If all the cards are reversed, start again, asking the client to focus more upon accessing help and guidance when shuffling the cards, rather than dwelling upon the problem.

NO WISDOM CARDS Readings lacking any Wisdom Cards often feel as if they are without power or direction. The client may not have deeply considered the question, or isn't seriously motivated, or isn't ready to hear the answer. You must judge such situations yourself and either instruct the client to reshuffle with greater concentration, or read for that person another day.

A predominance of Dialogue Cards means that the client is currently working through relationships and communications.

Keys to unlock the wisdom inside you

When you can't understand any card in a reading, try asking the relevant question to help unlock the innate wisdom within.

WISDOM CARDS

0	The Soul:	*Where are you seeking wisdom?*
I	The Decider:	*What is manifesting in your life?*
II	The Guardian:	*What is the source of your truth?*
III	The Shaper:	*What spiritual nurture is your soul seeking?*
IV	The Keeper:	*What is the source of your own authority?*
V	The Rememberer:	*What song is guiding you?*
VI	The Lover:	*Where is love in your life?*
VII	The Mover:	*Which energies need to be harnessed?*
VIII	The Empowerer:	*What power lies untapped in you?*
IX	The Counselor:	*What seeks to be born in the silence?*
X	The Spinner:	*What patterns are unfolding in your life?*
XI	The Balancer:	*What keeps you in balance with the universe?*
XII	The Dedicator:	*What duties arise from your beliefs?*
XIII	The Liberator:	*What do you need to let go of?*
XIV	The Mingler:	*What is experience teaching you?*
XV	The Challenger:	*How are you limiting yourself?*
XVI	The Changer:	*What old habits/structures have you outgrown?*
XVII	The Dreamer:	*What is the source of refreshment in your life?*
XVIII	The Imaginer:	*Which natural rhythms are out of harmony?*
XIX	The Protector:	*Who are you in your authentic self?*
XX	The Renewer:	*Where is transformation imminent in your life?*
XXI	The Perfecter:	*What is the story of your soul?*

STORY CARDS

1. Battle: *Where can you engage more strongly with life?*
2. Battle: *Where is reconciliation needed?*
3. Battle: *What sorrow/hurt is festering in your heart?*
4. Battle: *What opportunities for space and rest are offered?*
5. Battle: *How are previous thoughts and actions coming to roost?*
6. Battle: *What opportunity/initiation is being offered?*
7. Battle: *Whom are you seeking to deceive?*
8. Battle: *What attitudes are isolating you?*
9. Battle: *What freedoms and alternatives are offered?*
10. Battle: *What is the source of your greatest help?*
    Woman of Battle: *What changes are constellating now?*
    Warrior of Battle: *What requires your championship?*
    Queen of Battle: *What independent stand is required of you?*
    King of Battle: *What insights authorize you to act?*

1. Skill: *Where is the skill and enthusiasm in your life?*
2. Skill: *What unites your skills and goals?*
3. Skill: *What help is being offered?*
4. Skill: *How can you enjoy the fruits of your labors?*
5. Skill: *What is the kernel of truth at the problem's heart?*
6. Skill: *What is your true skill in life?*
7. Skill: *What do you need to defend resourcefully?*
8. Skill: *What reservations impede your free action?*
9. Skill: *Where are you giving away power?*
10. Skill: *Which tasks need to be delegated?*
    Woman of Skill: *In whom or what is your loyalty bestowed?*
    Warrior of Skill: *What provokes your passionate creativity?*
    Queen of Skill: *What does your common sense tell you?*
    King of Skill: *How are you using your skills to serve your community?*

1. Art: *How are you being called to receive and grow?*
2. Art: *Where is trust in your situation?*
3. Art: *What blocks a good outcome?*
4. Art: *What falsehoods and burdens are weighing you down?*
5. Art: *What can be saved from the situation?*
6. Art: *Which dreams, memories, and symbols give you life?*
7. Art: *Which is illusion, which is symbolically true?*
8. Art: *Where are your energies uselessly committed?*
9. Art: *What is your heart's desire?*
10. Art: *How can you share the blessing/gift?*
    Woman of Art: *Who or what supports your inner vision?*
    Warrior of Art: *Who or what kindles your dreaming soul?*
    Queen of Art: *Who or what nurtures your soul?*
    King of Art: *What action does your innate generosity dictate?*

1. Knowledge: *How is your spiritual treasure dispensing wisdom?*
2. Knowledge: *What strategies need a more playful approach?*
3. Knowledge: *How are you challenged to produce your best work?*
4. Knowledge: *What is being hoarded or coveted?*
5. Knowledge: *Where are respect and trust excluded?*
6. Knowledge: *What needs to be shared?*
7. Knowledge: *What continued effort is needed?*
8. Knowledge: *What needs to be assimilated still?*
9. Knowledge: *What is your gut instinct about things?*
10. Knowledge: *What solutions arise from your experience?*
    Woman of Knowledge: *Who or what is offering you advice?*
    Warrior of Knowledge: *Who or what can be trusted?*
    Queen of Knowledge: *Who or what is being woven in?*
    King of Knowledge: *What is the essential wisdom here?*

This has been our way: spring for plowing and sowing; summer for strengthening the crop; autumn for grain's ripeness and for reaping; winter for consuming its goodness.

LEBOR GABÁLA ERENN
(translation: Caitlín Matthews)

THE PATHWAYS OF THE YEAR

V

Finding the Hidden Treasures

As well as a tool for divination, the cards can also be used for tracking the story of our own souls. By meditating upon the images of the cards, we will kindle and connect with the knowing already inside us. This creates a living, oral network of wisdom that goes beyond the written word; by personally interrelating with the ancient knowledge, we recreate it within our own time. This method of meditation brings us into closer relationship with the wisdom of the ogham trees that appear in each of the Wisdom Cards, and enables us to encounter each of the characters and archetypes of the tradition.

The meditation sequence suggested on pages 137–143 takes a whole year, comprising the four Celtic seasons of Samhain, Imbolc, Beltane, and Lughnasa. It apportions each suit and its associated Wisdom Cards into seasonal sections (see page 52). Allow the changing seasons to reveal to you your own fallow, burgeoning, creative, and rewarding soul-phases. When the going gets tough and the cards you're working with seem to mirror your own difficulties, use the spreads in Chapter 4 to give you fresh insight. Draw out the cards that have qualities you most need and desire and add these to your meditations. Ask yourself the questions given in the Soul-Wisdom sections of the cards, or the questions in the quick reference guide on pages 130–131, to find new freedoms.

To give a whole year to meditation takes a high degree of commitment, but the rewards will more than make up for it. The Celtic tradition, like any path of wisdom, covers a lot of terrain and takes time and experience to understand fully. Follow the clues given to find the Four Treasures and then implement them in your own life.

Meditation Method

Meditation requires only your clear intention to enter stillness in order to step upon the pathway formed by the cards, a willingness to learn, a receptivity to change, and sufficient commitment to continue.

Allow roughly a half hour per session: this might be slightly longer or shorter. Practice for a minimum of two to three times a week. Be moderate but consistent in your meditation. If you're feeling unwell or under pressure, give yourself a break.

Practice in a quiet place. Sit where you can position the cards under consideration in clear view, without visual or physical strain. Breathe deeply, and let go of tension in your body, release troubles from your mind, and unclench any burdens and constraints. Be aware of the earth beneath you and the sky above you, and yourself in between. Start every session in this way.

On this course you will be entering the cards in meditation, interacting with their figures, scenes, and landscapes. This will involve dialogue: speaking, answering, and listening. Don't avoid this interaction: it is richly rewarding and will teach you more about the cards than a book ever can.

Keep a record of your findings: note the date, the cards you were working with, and the realizations you had. It doesn't have to be a full academic report. Feel free to make it as informal as you like: include poems, songs, relevant sketches, news-clippings, personal associations, funny observations, complaints, and triumphs.

Expectations and Support

I cannot prescribe what you will experience when you do this course. From my teaching experience, I know that the following concerns may arise:

1. "Am I doing it right?" There is no right way to experience what happens in meditation. Respect the evidence of both your inner and outer senses!
2. "Am I deluding myself?" Meditation experiences are often powerful. They push at the boundaries of our society's narrow attitude to reality, which allows flesh and blood to exist but which doubts the existence of the soul or anything unseen. The archetypes, figures, trees, and spirits of this deck all exist in their own right. If this bothers you, act "as if" they were real, until you learn to trust the evidence for yourself.
3. "My visualization skills are poor." To compensate, meditate using the full range of your senses, especially touch and hearing. What kinds of feelings, fears, exultations, and physical rushes of energy are you experiencing? These all show that you are visualizing successfully.
4. "I think I'm making this happen/imagining this." Imagination is a faculty of the soul: it views the unseen dimensions of reality, which are just as real as the physical world we inhabit. The images and metaphors of our dreams, poetry, and song, our intuitive pictures and impressions of states, conditions, and archetypes are the truest and most potent of gifts. Pay attention to your dreams, meditations, and mystical experiences – everyone has them.
5. "It's not going well. I feel upset/disturbed/vulnerable." You will have off-days when you should let up and do something ordinary, but don't ignore the feelings that emerge when you engage with certain cards: some will make you uneasy because they come close to states you personally exemplify. We all have "reversed cards" in our makeup. Get to know yourself with the help of the cards: this is the path to wisdom.
6. "I don't know what to do! Who can help me?" Figure out early on who your tarot allies are in this deck: ask the cards you are drawn to for help. Don't neglect your soul-friend – the one close human friend with whom you can discuss your most private, inner thoughts. You are not alone in the universe. Nature helps put things in perspective. You are a free soul and can make your own decisions without giving away your power to another.

The Ogham Trees and Substitutions

For the meditation sequence that follows, you will need a working knowledge of the ogham trees. The ogham trees are specific to the Celtic lands of northwest Europe, so readers outside this region will need to discover alternatives among their own indigenous trees. Although this breaks the mold of tradition, it is better that we each have a relationship with our own native trees, rather than working with species that have no meaning or relevance for us.

The following are suggestions to help your quest:

Ogham Tree	Substitute
Scots Pine	Conifers or needle-leafed trees
Gorse	Brightly flowering shrubs growing on heathland or poor soil
Heather	Low, clustering aromatic plants growing in poor soil or hilly areas
Aspen	Any tree whose leaves give the appearance of quivering
Yew	The longest-lived evergreen species of tree growing in your region
Birch	The first tree to put on leaf after the winter, or trees associated with cleansing
Rowan	Berry-bearing tree associated with magic
Ash	Tall, straight, leaf-shedding tree with seed-cases or pods
Alder	Water-loving, leaf-shedding trees
Willow	Trees that fringe rivers and creeks
Hawthorn	Flowering, berry-producing trees that herald summer
Oak	The strongest tree
Holly	Evergreens with shiny leaves
Hazel	Quick-growing, nut-bearing trees whose wood is useful
Apple	Fruit-bearing trees
Bramble	Thorny, rambling shrubs
Ivy	Creepers, climbers, lianas, and so on
Reed	Any reed, rush, or grass
Blackthorn	Spiny flowering trees or shrubs bearing fruit
Elder	Blossoming, berry-producing trees that grow anywhere

The Meditation Sequence

This meditation sequence requires you to have a working knowledge of the ogham trees (see pages 10–11, and opposite).

PREPARATORY SESSION

The preparatory meditation is upon the following two cards: 0 The Soul, and XXI The Perfecter.

Closing your eyes, enter the card of The Soul and stand before the holed stone, between the Yew and Birch trees. Make your own invocation as you prepare to journey into the reality of the cards to meet allies and to seek wisdom, perhaps something like this:

> *Before the doorway of the stone,*
> *I seek to pass the threshold bright,*
> *In search of wisdom's hidden might.*
> *Companions of the living light,*
> *Be near, that I go not alone!*

Pass through the hole in the stone and emerge on the other side of the picture where The Perfecter sits, surrounded by the Four Treasures. The Perfecter shows yourself as you can be, with the qualities and abilities that the sacred objects confer, with the ogham trees' wisdom at your disposal. This figure is, as yet, merely a promise. The only thing that is tangible is the breastplate that The Perfecter wears. Using this breastplate as a board, lay out each of the four cards upon which you are currently meditating.

THE ANNUAL SEQUENCE

Start your year of meditation at the relevant date. Let's say you are at July 3. Look up that date in the guide on pages 140–142. This is the time to explore Adventure of Art, Elopement of Art, King of Art, and XV The Challenger. The relevant ogham tree is Hazel. Before you meditate, study each card in turn until you're familiar with the backgrounds and meanings. If possible (but not essential), try to get a slip of Hazel or a regional substitute to hold while you meditate. Now you are ready to meditate with the cards and the tree as your teachers.

In the center of the breastplate/board on The Perfecter's breast, you see the ogham tree – Hazel – growing. Be aware of the letter of the alphabet that the tree represents: ask the tree itself for teaching about this. Greet the tree in silence. Be present with it, spirit to spirit. Listen to its wisdom. If you haven't got an actual leaf or twig, in meditation visualize yourself plucking one from the tree growing before you. This is your talisman and passport for your journey.

Now enter the card of the King of Art, who is the God Lugh. Meet and greet him, asking any questions to clarify your understanding. Ask him to take you to the other cards in the set, as a guide and companion. He will take you to the Adventure of Art and Elopement of Art, where you can, in turn, ask questions of the characters within those scenes. Finally, King of Art will take you into the card of XV The Challenger. This card shows two scenes: the one above shows the soul's ancestral struggle, the one below shows the God Cernunnos. Ask King of Art which scene is appropriate to visit first.

At any point in the meditation, should you be challenged or feel uncertain, hold or visualize the sprig of the ogham tree and ask the tree-spirit to help or guard you. If you've spent meaningful amounts of time with the Hazel tree, you will find yourself truly companioned.

At the end of each session of meditation, return to the scene of The Perfecter. Say farewell to the tree upon whose related cards you've been meditating and return to the scene of The Soul. Create another invocation to return you to your own time and place.

Something like this invocation would be appropriate:

> *From treasure realms of seed and tree,*
> *Beyond the curtain of the night,*
> *I come companioned by the light*
> *Of visions true and wisdom's might,*
> *To tread my soul-path willingly.*

The meditation sequence I've just described will not happen all in one session, of course. You can return over the course of the weeks' sessions on each set of cards, gradually building up your experience. As you finish each set's meditation, return to the ogham tree growing from The Perfecter's breast: lay the leaf, twig, or sprig you took from that tree upon the letter to which it corresponds on one of the Four Treasures. In the case of Hazel, you will lay your sprig upon the four-stroked ogham letter in the cauldron. When you begin the next set, visualize The Perfecter's breast as clear, ready for the next tree.

GUIDELINES FOR EACH SESSION

1. Enter stillness.
2. Enter The Soul card and proceed to The Perfecter.
3. Interact with the ogham tree of the card-set.
4. See the card-set of your session displayed upon The Perfecter's breastplate.
5. Enter and meet the Court Card – the Woman, Warrior, Queen, or King. You have a choice of Court Card in the final session of each seasonal suit. Choose any Court Card you've already encountered.
6. A Court Card guides you through the two Story Cards in each set. Ask whatever questions you wish.
7. Enter the Wisdom Card and be guided by the Court Card.
8. Say farewell to all the scenes you've entered. Return to The Perfecter.
9. If you have finished a card-set, then lay the sprig of the tree upon the corresponding letter of the appropriate Treasure in The Perfecter scene.
10. Return via The Soul card entrance – the two trees and holed stone – to your own time and place. Record your findings.

The Annual Sequence

Start your year of meditation at the relevant date.

SAMHAIN — SEASON OF WINTER

November 1
I Decider of Will
Augury of Battle
Dialogue of Battle
Woman of Battle

OGHAM TREE: *Scots Pine*
OGHAM TITLE/LETTER: *Ailim/A*

November 22
V Rememberer of Lore
Courtship of Battle
Judgment of Battle
Warrior of Battle

OGHAM TREE: *Gorse*
OGHAM TITLE/LETTER: *Ohn/O*

December 13
IX Counsellor of Truth
Combat of Battle
Foundation of Battle
Queen of Battle

OGHAM TREE: *Heather*
OGHAM TITLE/LETTER: *Ur/U*

January 4
XIII Liberator of Devotion
Adventure of Battle
Elopement of Battle
King of Battle

OGHAM TREE: *Aspen*
OGHAM TITLE/LETTER: *Eodha/E*

January 18
XVII Dreamer of Growth
Revelation of Battle
Quest of Battle
The Battle Court Card of your choice

OGHAM TREE: *Yew*
OGHAM TITLE/LETTER: *Ioho/I*

Meditate upon the Sword and upon the letters that Scots Pine, Gorse, Heather, Aspen, and Yew have revealed to you. Create your own reading, based upon the lessons you've learnt this winter.

IMBOLC — SEASON OF SPRING

February 1
II Guardian of Truth
Augury of Skill
Dialogue of Skill
Woman of Skill

OGHAM TREE: *Birch*
OGHAM TITLE/LETTER: *Beith/B*

February 22
VI Lover of Devotion
Courtship of Skill
Judgment of Skill
Warrior of Skill

OGHAM TREE: *Rowan*
OGHAM TITLE/LETTER: *Luis/L*

March 1
X Spinner of Growth
Combat of Skill
Foundation of Skill
Queen of Skill

OGHAM TREE: *Ash*
OGHAM TITLE/LETTER: *Nion/N*

April 5
XIV Mingler of Energy
Adventure of Skill
Elopement of Skill
King of Skill

OGHAM TREE: *Alder*
OGHAM TITLE/LETTER: *Fearn/F*

April 19
XVIII Imaginer of Harmony
Revelation of Skill
Quest of Skill
The Skill Court Card of your choice

OGHAM TREE: *Willow*
OGHAM TITLE/LETTER: *Saille/S*

Meditate upon the Spear and upon the letters that Birch, Rowan, Ash, Alder, and Willow have revealed to you. Create your own reading, based upon the lessons you've learned this spring.

BELTANE — SEASON OF SUMMER

May 1
III Shaper of Growth
Augury of Art
Dialogue of Art
Woman of Art

OGHAM TREE: *Hawthorn*
OGHAM TITLE/LETTER: *Huathe/H*

May 22
VII Mover of Energy
Courtship of Art
Judgment of Art
Warrior of Art

OGHAM TREE: *Oak*
OGHAM TITLE/LETTER: *Duir/D*

June 12
XI Balancer of Harmony
Combat of Art
Foundation of Art
Queen of Art

OGHAM TREE: *Holly*
OGHAM TITLE/LETTER: *Tinne/T*

July 3
XV Challenger of Will
Adventure of Art
Elopement of Art
King of Art

OGHAM TREE: *Hazel*
OGHAM TITLE/LETTER: *Coll/C*

July 19
XIX Protector of Lore
Revelation of Art
Quest of Art
The Art Court Card of your choice

OGHAM TREE: *Apple*
OGHAM TITLE/LETTER: *Quert/Q or P or CW*

Meditate upon the Cauldron and upon the letters that Hawthorn, Oak, Holly, Hazel, and Apple have shown to you. Create your own reading, based upon the lessons you've learned this summer.

LUGHNASA — SEASON OF FALL

August 1
IV Keeper of Harmony
Augury of Knowledge
Dialogue of Knowledge
Woman of Knowledge

OGHAM TREE: *Bramble*
OGHAM TITLE/LETTER: *Muin/M*

August 22
VIII Empowerer of Will
Courtship of Knowledge
Judgment of Knowledge
Warrior of Knowledge

OGHAM TREE: *Ivy*
OGHAM TITLE/LETTER: *Gort/G*

September 11
XII Dedicator of Lore
Combat of Knowledge
Foundation of Knowledge
Queen of Knowledge

OGHAM TREE: *Reed*
OGHAM TITLE/LETTER: *Ngetal/Ng*

October 2
XVI Changer of Truth
Adventure of Knowledge
Elopement of Knowledge
King of Knowledge

OGHAM TREE: *Blackthorn*
OGHAM TITLE/LETTER: *Straif/Str or Z*

October 19
XX Renewer of Devotion
Revelation of Knowledge
Quest of Knowledge
The Knowledge Court Card of your choice

OGHAM TREE: *Elder*
OGHAM TITLE/LETTER: *Ruis/R*

Meditate upon the Stone and upon the letters that Bramble, Ivy, Reed, Blackthorn, and Elder have shown to you. Create your own reading, based upon the lessons you've learned this fall.

Final Session

Finish your year's meditation by laying out the whole deck in a large circle, in the annual sequence given on pages 140–142, putting 0 The Soul and XXI The Perfecter in the center.

Review your journey through each season. In your final meditation, enter the card of The Perfecter and take his place, with the Four Treasures around you. Ask each of the Treasures to send a card of its own suit to act as soul-friends. You may choose the card of each suit that was of most help to you over this year. Or draw them unseen from the deck, which has been previously sorted into each of the suits.

Welcome each card. As you do so, each of the Treasures is taken into the scene of its respective suit card. Each of these cards now becomes a part of your breastplate. Return with the knowledge that you can, in times of need, call upon the powers that are a part of The Perfecter. Read the four suit cards in the normal way on your return.

By meditating upon the whole sequence, you will discover a great deal about the cards and the wisdom they hold for you, especially from the ogham trees under whose branches you have stood and listened. Your meditation will enable your readings for yourself and others to become highly sensitive, because you will have entered each of these scenes for yourself and understood the deeper wisdom, which is the real treasure, of the Celtic tradition.

0 THE SOUL

XXI THE PERFECTER

Resources

Hallowquest Newsletter To receive details of forthcoming courses, tours, events, and books of Caitlín & John Matthews, please write to Caitlín Matthews, BCM Hallowquest, London WC1N 3XX, UK. For a sample copy of the quarterly newsletter send 8 first class stamps (within UK) or $5 US bill. No foreign checks please. Also see their website at www.hallowquest.org.uk

Foundation For Inspirational And Oracular Studies promotes the sacred arts, including those of divination, shamanism, healing, and inspirational art. Its "Walkers Between the Worlds" courses are led by Caitlín & John Matthews and Felicity Wombwell, providing practical training opportunities to learn the ancestral sacred arts by oral and experiential means. Send an SAE (in UK) or 2 international reply-paid coupons (outside UK) to FÍOS, BCM Hallowquest, London WC1N 3XX, UK.

Bibliography

Books were printed in London, unless stated otherwise.

Auraicept na n-Eces ed. George Calder, Four Courts Press, Dublin, 1995
Coombes, Allen J. *Trees: A Visual Guide to Over 500 Species of Tree from Around the World,* Dorling Kindersley, 1992
Cross, T.P. & Slover, C.H. *Ancient Irish Tales,* Figgis, Dublin, 1936
Davidson, Hilda Ellis ed. *The Seer in Celtic and Other Traditions,* John Donaldson, Edinburgh, 1989
Gray, W.G. *Magical Ritual Methods,* Helios Books, Toddington, 1969
Greer, Mary *Tarot for Yourself,* Newcastle Publishing Co., North Hollywood, 1984
Gregory, Lady *Cuchulain of Muirthemne,* Colin Smythe, Gerrard's Cross, 1970
Gregory, Lady *Gods & Fighting Men,* Colin Smythe, Gerrard's Cross, 1970
Kirk, Robert *The Secret Commonwealth,* ed. Stewart Sanderson, D.S. Brewer, Cambridge, 1976
Mabey, Richard *Flora Britannica,* Sinclair-Stevenson, 1996
Macmanus, Damian *A Guide to Ogam,* Maynooth, An Sagart, 1991
The Mabinogion ed. Lady Charlotte Guest, Ballantyne, Edinburgh, 1910
Matthews, Caitlín *Arthur and the Sovereignty of Britain,* Arkana, 1989
Matthews, Caitlín *The Celtic Book of the Dead* (ill. Danuta Meyer), Thorsons, 1992
Matthews, Caitlín *Celtic Devotional,* Godsfield Press, New Alresford, 1996
Matthews, Caitlín *The Celtic Spirit,* Harper, San Francisco, 1999
Matthews, Caitlín *Elements of Celtic Tradition,* Element Books, Shaftesbury, 1989
Matthews, Caitlín *In Search of Woman's Passionate Soul: Revealing the Daimon Lover Within,* Element Books, Shaftesbury, 1997
Matthews, Caitlín *Mabon & the Mysteries of Britain,* Arkana, 1987
Matthews, Caitlín *The One Story Worth the Telling,* Harper, San Francisco, 2000, forthcoming.
Matthews, Caitlín *Singing the Soul Back Home: Shamanism in Daily Life,* Element Books, Shaftesbury, 1996
Matthews, Caitlín & John *The Arthurian Tarot* (ill. Miranda Gray), HarperCollins, 1990
Matthews, Caitlín & John *Encyclopedia of Celtic Wisdom: A Celtic Shaman's Sourcebook,* Element Books, Shaftesbury, 1994
Matthews, Caitlín & John *Hallowquest: The Arthurian Tarot Course,* HarperCollins, 1997
Matthews, John *The Bardic Source Book,* Cassell, 1998
Matthews, John ed. *A Celtic Reader,* Thorsons, 1995
Matthews, John *The Celtic Shaman's Pack* (ill. Chesca Potter), Element Books, Shaftesbury, 1996
Matthews, John ed. *The Druid Source Book,* Cassell, 1997
Matthews, John ed. *The Seer's Source Book,* Cassell, 1999
Matthews, John *Taliesin: Shamanism and the Bardic Mysteries in Britain and Ireland,* Aquarian, 1991
Matthews, John ed. *The World Atlas of Divination,* Rider, 1992
Nagy, Joseph F. *The Wisdom of the Outlaw,* Berkeley, University of California Press, 1985
Pennick, Nigel *The Secret Lore of Runes and Other Ancient Alphabets,* Rider, 1991
Pollack, Rachel & Matthews, Caitlín, *Tarot Tales,* Ace, New York, 1996
Ross, Anne & Robins, Don *The Life and Death of a Druid Prince,* Rider, 1989
Stewart, R.J. & Matthews, John *Merlin Through the Ages,* Blandford, 1995
Sutherland, Elizabeth *Ravens and Black Rain,* Constable, 1985
Trioedd Ynys Prydein (The Welsh Triads) ed. Rachel Bromwich, University of Wales Press, Cardiff, 1961